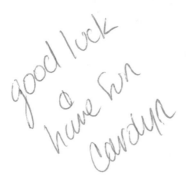

YOU CAN'T WIN
IF YOU DON'T ENTER

by
Carolyn Wilman

ISBN :1-4196-1328-6
Library of Congress Control Number : 2005908280

To order additional copies, please contact us.
Imagination Edge Inc.
www.contestqueen.com
1.866.231.6676
orders@contestqueen.com

DEDICATION

For all those who helped me make my dreams come true:
Mom, Dad, Laura, Ryan, Len, Piri and especially Craig and Nicole.
Thank you for helping me become a *winner*!

In memoriam:
Lynn Marie Banks Goutbeck
co-author of Winning Ways
March 10, 1952 - April 28, 2005

ACKNOWLEDGEMENTS

I would like to extend my deepest thanks to all those who helped me write this book and make it a success.

Qué Banh, Dominique Belisle, Bob Blumer, Roman Bodnarchuk, Stephen Bush, Costa Caruso, Kimberly Clancy, D'Arcy Emery, John Findley, Lynn Goutbeck, Bob Gunther, Joe Head, Norah Higgerty, Marc Gagnon, Pat Galarneau-Trithart, Sylvia Gold, Lynn Goutbeck, Corrine Katz, François Lane, David Larade, Vincent Lavoie, Michael Lipton, Michael Losier, Duncan McCready, Richard Meltzer, Wayne Mouland, Lori Novak, Brenda Pritchard, Melanie Rockett, Dave Rossborough, Shannon Shoemaker, Ingrid & Tom Stamatson, Sacha Sylvain, Tony Sylvain, Barb Taylor, Susan Vogt, James Walker, Patrick, Watson and all my fellow contestors who are now friends and those kind enough to let me include their stories: Audrey, Bea, Erin, Fred, Kevin, Lois, Mary, Susan B., Susan S. and Wanda.

I want to give an extra special thank you to Scott Cruickshank who during our interview stated, "You can't win if you don't enter." and I knew it was to be the name of this book.

To Kevin Amery, who patiently edited and reedited this book.

And finally, Craig Borysowich, my husband, who wrote the chapter Spyware, Viruses and Spam OH MY! Thank you for providing all the information technology know-how to make this book complete.

TABLE OF CONTENTS

Forward **9**

Introduction **11**

Why Run a Contest? **25**

Rules and Regulations **35**

Five Ways to Enter **41**

My Internet Contesting System **67**

Contesting Software **85**

Join an Online Community **97**

Spyware, Viruses and Spam, OH MY! **105**

You're a Winner! **121**

Scams **131**

Contest Development and Management Companies **145**

Attracting Luck **165**

Conclusion **191**

Recommended Reading **193**

FORWARD

You'd think that after all these years, and all the information about sweepstakes you can find in books and on the Internet, there would be nothing more to say. WRONG! As the technology continues to change and as sweepstakes evolve, there are more questions than ever before… that's because there are more ways to enter, different kinds of sweeps, more prizes up for grabs, and more places to find sweepstakes than in all previous decades combined. There are also more scams.

Even though Carolyn and I live across the country from one another, we first met on the telephone. I have been contesting for many years and because of my books and contest newsletter I often get calls "out of the blue." I get so used to hearing the same questions again and again that I tend to "tune out." And I get so immersed in telling people about contests I often get too tired to enter for myself! From the very first, Carolyn's call was different. She was so amazingly enthusiastic! She started sharing information on how she was winning… and by golly, she was inspiring! Over the months she continued to call and email and share… until finally, we got to meet in person. No surprise, Carolyn is as enthusiastic and vivacious in person as she is over the phone.

I was very interested to see if Carolyn had anything new to say on the topic. I wasn't disappointed. Carolyn wrote this book with the specific intention of giving her readers hands-on and highly practical information about the hobby of sweepstaking. From interviews with the people who run some of the largest sweepstakes in the country, to her personal experiences of winning. From encouraging you to go high tech and get in on text messaging sweeps to giving you great information about how to avoid scams and stay safe on the Internet… it is all there, and more!

Anyone who is interested in the hobby of sweepstaking will benefit from the knowledge Carolyn shares. Her suggestions are geared to all levels of contestors, from the beginner who has only thought about entering… to the advanced hobbyist who has been winning for years.

AND she speaks from experience. Like many of us Carolyn stumbled upon sweepstaking as a hobby, by winning one sweep. That win sparked her interest and she kept on entering. The more she entered… the more she won. Carolyn had discovered for herself… you can't win if you don't enter! She is now a seasoned contest enthusiast who wins at least once or twice a week every week of the year. Carolyn takes the hobby of sweepstaking very seriously and she is truly Canada's Contest Queen!

Everything in this book is presented in Carolyn's enthusiastic style. She LOVES sweepstaking. She LOVES winning. And even more she LOVES sharing the hobby of sweepstaking with everyone she meets.

I am thrilled to introduce you to Carolyn's book and to the results you can achieve in reading and following the ideas she has presented. As you find yourself winning, please do others around you the ultimate favor—share the ideas and the enthusiasm in this book so that they too, can experience the thrill of being a winner!

Melanie Rockett

Author of the books *Contest Guru's Guide to Winning Sweepstakes*; *Winning Ways*; publisher of the ContestGuru.com and ProofPositive.com websites; and editor of the very sporadic *Contest News* newsletter.

"Everything in life is luck."
Donald Trump

INTRODUCTION

I *love* entering contests. I get such a thrill out of finding new ones and reading about all the different prizes that I could win, I get butterflies in my stomach. I daydream about all the various trips I could take, the cars I could drive, or what I wo mnuld spend the cash on. I *love* getting notified I won a prize. I get all bubbly inside and I grin from ear-to-ear for hours. ***I am passionate about contesting.***

How Winning Changed My Life
I have good reason to feel this way. Contesting has actually changed the course of my life. Winning prizes back in 1991 lead to going on a trip to Barbados with my mom... and to the first date I had with my husband.

It was early December 1990 and a popular Toronto radio station, CHFI 98.1FM, was broadcasting their morning show for a week in Simpson's department store window. I worked in a nearby office tower and every day I would stop to watch and listen. One morning, they gave away prize packs including tickets to the Ice Capades and a gift certificate for Fiorio, a trendy hair salon, to the first person that could show them a photo of their children. I whipped open my wallet and flashed the photo of my little cousins, winning the prize pack.

My mom had been home with the flu so when I got home I gave her the gift certificate to the hair salon. (All you ladies will understand; I had been having my hair cut by the same hairstylist for five years - almost twenty years now - and would never get my hair done anywhere else *even if I won it*!) We decided when she felt better we would spend the day together; going to the salon, having lunch and Christmas shopping downtown.

You Can't Win If You Don't Enter

The restaurant we had lunch at that day was giving away a trip to Barbados. As we left the restaurant, I realized I forgot to get the contest ballots. I made Mom wait as I ran back inside. When I returned I told her I would fill the forms out later, since the restaurant was close to my office. I said: "If I win I'll take you and if you win you'll take me!"

On December 24th we were all at home, wrapping gifts in the living room, when the phone rang. Mom went into the kitchen to answer the call. I could only hear her side of the conversation. The woman identified herself and stated my mom may have won a trip. Mom really doesn't like telemarketers and nearly couldn't figure out what was going on, but since it was Christmas she decided not to hang up right away. The woman asked my mom, "Where is Barbados?" My Mom nearly said she didn't know. Instead, she said, "In the Caribbean." She was told she did in fact win the trip and the travel agency would contact her in January to make all the arrangements. My Mom was confused and asked, "How did I win this trip?" I heard that and screamed, "We won! We won!" The woman asked her; "Didn't you fill out a ballot?" My mom said; "I think one of my kids entered me" as I jumped up and down around her.

TIP: Remember to tell your friends and family when you have entered them in contests, so if they win they don't inadvertently lose the prize or disqualify themselves.

We went the following April. It was really special to spend a whole week alone with my mom -- we had the best time and we learned a lot about each other. I would love to win another trip so that my mom, my daughter and I can go together.

TIP: If you wish to take children on the trip, read the rules and check out the destination's website to ensure children are allowed at the resort or hotel. It would be a shame to try and win a vacation for the family, only to discover that only you and your partner can go.

So that's how I won the trip to Barbados, but I know some of you are wondering about that first date with my husband. Well, I also won those four tickets to the Ice Capades. I gave away one set to a girlfriend in my office. I then started inviting friends to see who would like to go with me. I must have invited thirty people - no one wanted to go. One day I was speaking to Craig, who at the time was a business acquaintance, and asked him to go with me. Unlike those thirty other people, *he* said yes. We had a great time. *I* thought I had made a new friend; *he* says it was our first date and I just didn't know it. We just celebrated our 10th wedding anniversary. Would we have begun a true friendship had I not won those tickets? Who knows?

My Best Win—EVER!

I continued to contest sporadically until I read an article that led me to become a "contestor." (*For Definitions see NOTE at end of Introduction.*) At the time, I had been unemployed for the longest period I have ever experienced in my professional life. One night I was lying in bed, reading the August 2001 copy of Reader's Digest, when I came across an article called "Get in the Winner's Circle! Tips from a contest junkie who's proven that the best things in life *are* free" by Barb Taylor. I read and reread that article and as I did I made a decision—from then on, I would *win* all the things I wanted in life; like a new car!

Get in the Winner's Circle!

Tips from a contest junkie who's proven that the best things in life *are* free

by Barb Taylor
From Calgary Herald

Vacations in Italy. Hawaii and Mexico. Doing rolls in a stunt plane or being whisked off in a limousine for a night of wining, dining and theatre. Hardly the lifestyle you'd expect for an average-income family of four living in a duplex and driving a rusty old Volvo. Certainly not the lifestyle we envisioned when I left my teaching job 12 years ago to become a stay-at-home mom.

Our magical life began in 1988 after a sleepless night spent attending to our newborn son. The following day I entered a contest sponsored by a local radio station, inviting listeners to send letters to Santa. I pleaded with Santa for one night of uninterrupted sleep. My entry was selected for a one-week trip to Lake Tahoe from radio station CJAY 92. I was hooked.

Now I enter lots of contests, anywhere from 200 to 300 a year. I find out about them while shopping for groceries, listening to the radio, browsing through magazines and regularly perusing a contest newsletter to which I subscribe. Over the years, I've spent three to four hours a week researching new contests and filling out forms.

But the hard work has paid off. I averaged $10,000 in annual winnings; I've won two Dirt Devils through the Safeway Score & Win; and I've gone on a total of

14 major trips thanks to this winning hobby. My writing talents have won me a fair share of prizes as well, everything from a pair of $1,000 earrings for a local magazine's limerick contest to a pair of lift tickets for a *Calgary Herald*-sponsored Ski Memories contest.

Our winnings have also included clothing, appliances, a backyard barbecue and a patio set. We rarely pay to go to a movie or theatrical production. We frequently dine on gift certificates we have won. The luxuries our income doesn't provide for, my contesting does. Even our children get in on the act and have won a bike, a skateboard and passes to local attractions.

We've watched beautiful sunsets in Maui (courtesy of the Lite 96 jet) and Oahu (thanks to KissFM), walked the Freedom Trail in Boston (Calgary Co-op supermarket and Kraft foods), and even sent my in-laws to Scotland (a cross-Canada random draw from United Distillers). Will it ever end? Not as long as I can fill out an entry for or clip a Universal Product Code, or UPC as it's known (the bar code on products you buy).

Most of the trips I have won fall into the middle "good-and besides it's free" category. While not all-inclusive, your major costs of airfare and accommodation are covered. You stay in above average accommodation, usually a three-star hotel. You are generally responsible for your own meals, spending money and, occasionally, airport taxes. Trips we've won in this category included a one-week trip to San José del Cabo at the tip of Mexico's Baja peninsula. We enjoyed beautiful, uncrowded beaches, drinkable water, and simple but clean accommodations.

My husband and I experienced our "dream come true" trip courtesy of a local real-estate developer. By dropping off three entry forms at a tour of show homes, we won a one-week trip to Florence, which included stopovers in Paris and London. In Florence, we stayed at the Hotel Brunelleschi in a $650-a-night room that had floor-to-ceiling louvered windows opening onto a tiny flowered courtyard. We had a breathtaking view of the Duomo and the Campanile.

Nowadays, friends often rub my arm for luck before they head off to buy their lottery tickets. I can only shake my head in wonder - I've never won anything in a lottery.

So, you must be wondering, how do I do it? In the world of contesting, luck really has nothing to do with it: It all comes down to effort and persistence. For every contest I win, there are 100 I've lost. Here are some suggestions to put the odds in your favour:

DO

☑ Pick free contests. These are usually drawbox contests and can be found in grocery stores and other businesses. Radio and television phone-in contests also cost nothing to enter.

☑ Also, pick the "better odds" contest: Look for contests that have a limited contesting area, offer lots of prizes, require you to "do something" (write a story, solve a puzzle), or that run for a short time span.

☑ Enter often. If it's a "better odds" contest, I'll enter five to 20 times. Try to space your entry mailings throughout the length of the contest's running.

☑ Collect UPCs. Remember that hand-drawn facsimiles are usually accepted in mail-in

16

contests, and believe me, they really work. I've won many contests using hand-drawn facsimiles.

☑ Subscribe to a newsletter detailing currently running contests. A good one is the Canadian Contest Newsletter, P.O. Box 776, Stn. U, Etobicoke, Ont. M8Z 5P9. On the web, you can find them at: www.canadian.contests.com.

DON'T

☒ Swipe the entry pads and then stuff the draw box. Getting greedy may get you disqualified for taking unfair advantage.

☒ Don't try to win more than once a month on a given radio station. If you make a nuisance of yourself by trying to win every prize offered, you lower your chances of winning something you really want.

☒ Don't waste money sending in dozens, or hundreds, of entries to a contest that gives away only one prize. This is a quick road to contest burnout.

☒ Don't get scammed! If you've won a contest you haven't entered—beware! If you have to be earning $40,000 a year and are required to attend a sales presentation—think twice!

☒ Don't send money to receive a prize—*ever*.

Reprinted with permission from the August 2001 Reader's Digest.

NOTE: The website address and mailing address listed in the article for the Canadian Contest Newsletter have since changed to:
www.canadiancontests.com

You Can't Win If You Don't Enter

Canadian Contests Newsletter
P.O. Box 23066, RPO McGillivray
Winnipeg, MB R3T 5S3

I began my contesting career by surfing the web, and discovered an entire community of people who enter contests as a hobby. I joined a few groups, signed up to a couple of newsletters and through trial and error came up with an Internet-based contest entering system that *works*. How do I know my system works? My results, of course -- I consistently win 5-10+ contests every month, month after month. I even had a month where I had *33 wins*!

I am so passionate about contesting and excited about winning, I decided to write this book after about the 100th person asked me what my secret was to winning so much. I knew I was on to something with the system I had developed over the past few years and I wanted to share my discoveries, ideas, thoughts and enthusiasm with others.

Then someone asked me, why would I give all my secrets away? Wouldn't teaching others how to be successful contestors decrease my odds of winning? It was a tough question....

I was contemplating whether or not I should continue to write the book while driving to a friend's house. On the way I passed a church. The service announcement board out front said "You Can't Lose Helping Others Win". That clinched it -- I thought, "That message is for me! God is telling me it is OK to write the book!"

In my book, I will cover everything from how I began, the ins and outs of the five ways to enter sweepstakes, the Internet Contesting System I have developed over years of entering (and entering and entering...), stories from fellow contestors, what pitfalls to avoid along with many tips and tricks to increase your odds of winning.

In the past, most books on the hobby of contesting focused on only three methods of entering; in-person, phone-in and mail-in. But this left out the field of Internet and mobile phone contests, which together are the newest, fastest growing, and easiest to enter form of contesting available today. I have focused this book on the online method of entering contests. When I began entering contests on a daily basis there was no single source of contesting information in Canada. My goal is to make this book (and the online resources on my website— www.contestqueen.com) a hub of all the contesting resources available today. With all this information at your fingertips, you can choose which methods of entry you want to participate in, which groups and forums you may want to join, and what types of contests you want to enter.

I feel contesting is one of the best hobbies around and I hope you will feel the same way after your first win. By reading this book and putting into practice the many ideas, tips and tricks included within, I hope you can enjoy the hobby of contesting as much as I do.

con·testor (kŏn′tĕst′ər)
n.   1) One who enters contests, sweepstakes, competitions, lotteries and raffles.

NOTE: You may have noticed that throughout this book I have spelled the word contestor with an OR as opposed to an ER. There is a reason for this. I created the word contestor because the proper definition of a contester is someone who is protesting or disputing something. We're trying to win cars and big-screen TVs here, not contest a will!

con·testing (kŏn′tĕst′)
v.   1) The act of entering contests.

con·test (kŏn′tĕst′)
n.   1) A struggle for superiority or victory between rivals.
2) A competition, especially one in which entrants perform separately and are rated by judges. See Synonyms at <u>conflict</u>.
con·test·ed, con·test·ing, con·tests (kən′tĕst′) (kŏn′tĕst′)

v. tr.   1) To compete or strive for.

2) To call into question and take an active stand against; dispute or challenge: **contest a will.** See Synonyms at oppose.

v. intr. 1) To struggle or compete; contend: **contested with** other bidders for the antique. Probably from French *conteste*, from *contester*, to dispute, from Old French, to call to witness, from Latin *contestari : com-,* com- + *testis, witness*; see trei - in Appendix I.

con·test a·ble *adj.*

con tes·ta tion (kŏn'tĕ-stā'shən) *n.*

con·test er *n.*

con·tes·tant (kən-tĕs'tənt, kŏn'tĕs'tənt)
n. 1) One taking part in a contest; a competitor.
2) One that contests or disputes something, such as an election or a will.

Copyright © 2000 by Houghton Mifflin Company. Adapted and reproduced by permission from the *American Heritage Dictionary of the English Language, Fourth Edition.*

My Winning Streak

On a very cold gray day in January, I got the email that every contestor waits for: Congratulations! Your name has been drawn for the **Grand Prize**, Trip for two to L.A. and dinner with/prepared by Bob Blumer, in **Meyer's "The Surreal Meal" contest**, sponsored by Alliance Atlantis Broadcasting Inc. and Meyer Canada Inc. (Along with the trip to L.A., I received an eight piece set of Meyer Anolon cookware and $500 Canadian spending money.)

TIP: You can collect air miles or points on the flights you have won. Each person must have their own account to maximize the free rewards on top of a win.

Craig and I arranged to take the trip in March. We arrived at the airport on Thursday morning and met our chaperone from Alliance Atlantis. (They need to ensure that their show's hosts are protected from crazy contestors.) I mentioned it had been a slow month and I had not won a single thing. We got to L.A. and discovered we had two phone messages; one from my Dad and one from my step-mother. Due to the time difference I could not call until Friday morning. When I called, my step-mother said "Are you sitting down?" I was expecting bad news. She then proceeded to tell me my niece won a trip for four to New York City!

At the beginning of the year I told my step-sister, I was going to start entering my niece and nephew in the contests for children. I thought they would enjoy receiving a neat new toy or DVD in the mail. Little did I know their first win would be the biggest thing I have ever won. (I consider it a win even though I don't get the prize because I did the entering.) I was so happy for them since they had never been on a family vacation and they were now going on the trip of a lifetime.

We then proceeded to have an amazing time in L.A. We arrived at Bob's home in the Hollywood hills at 8:00pm on Friday evening. He had called me a few weeks before the trip to discuss the menu. We agreed he would make us recipes from his upcoming cookbook *Surreal Gourmet Bites: show-stoppers and conversation starters*. Bob is also an oenophile so each course was paired with a selection from his extensive private wine collection. He is a wonderful host. Craig and I felt as if we had gone to a friend's home for dinner. I went out and purchased his new book when it was released so I could continue to enjoy his creations and share them with my family and friends.

NOTE: There are no photos of our evening with Bob in this book. It is important to read all the documents you sign with regards to a contest win. The contest prize waiver stated all photos taken during our evening are for personal use only and cannot be published. I can publish other photos of us taken that weekend.

We arrived home late Sunday night, tired, happy and feeling lucky that we had such a memorable long weekend. As a contestor you never know how long a dry spell will last or how long a winning streak will continue. At 10:00am Monday morning Craig got a phone call from a local radio station. He won a two-week European holiday - a nine country, fourteen day bus tour. He was shocked.

We went to Europe that September. The trip was with a tour company that specialized in youth groups 18-35. It was fast paced and had a party atmosphere. Being up late every night, getting up early every morning and running around a new city almost daily took its toll on me by the end of the vacation. I came home with a terrible cold, having sadly discovered I wasn't 21 anymore and couldn't keep up the pace I used to. No wonder they say 18-35! It's really tough on those of us over 35.

TIP: If one half of the couple is under 35 and the other is over, the older person can sign a waiver stating you understand the tour is designed for "young" people.

We visited London, Amsterdam, the Rhine Valley, Munich, Innsbruck, Hofgarten, Venice, Rome, Florence, Lucerne, Paris and then back to London. What a vacation! The two surprise bonuses of the tour were arriving in Munich on opening day of Oktoberfest (Who knew

Oktoberfest started in September?) and seeing the last 10 minutes of Pope John Paul II's Wednesday morning sermon in Rome.

The highlight of the vacation for me was the evening trip up the Eiffel Tower. I have always wanted to go to Paris, and standing on the upper deck, hugging Craig and looking over the lights of Paris as the tower twinkled was absolutely magical. I never felt luckier in my life!

Our best adventure on the tour was the morning we had a $100 breakfast.
It was the second last day of the trip and we were in Paris. After a brief tour of a perfumery, we found ourselves outside of the Opera House. We were hungry and decided to have a bite to eat, and were tired of eating small, quick breakfasts. Looking around we noticed Le Café de la Paix, Paris' most famous restaurant. (Embarrassingly, I did not recognize the name. Craig did recognize the name, remembering many world famous chefs began their careers in that very café.) We entered from the street entrance and I was thinking we may sit outside. Craig and I discussed our eating options with the Maitre D', and decided we would like to have the breakfast buffet. They sat us inside in a booth opposite the

hotel entrance. As we waited for our tea and coffee to arrive we noticed several very well dressed people come into the restaurant. Then we went to the buffet. I have never seen a buffet like this in my life! There were breads and cheeses from all over the world, twenty different kinds of fresh fruit, four types of fresh fruit juice, and the best scrambled eggs I have ever eaten. They even had an entire section of Japanese specialties. When I came back to the table I said to Craig, "I don't think we want to know what breakfast is going to cost us." We sat for an hour relaxing, eating, deciding what were going to see that afternoon and soaking in the atmosphere. When the bill arrived it was €64. It was worth every penny!

Many people ask me when I have time to enter so many contests. I have to quote R.J. Ward from a sign we found in the Tinker Town Museum just outside Santa Fe, NM.

TIP: For contests that offer trips as a prize, if the entry parameters are one per household, enter the person with the most flexible travel schedule. Most trips are non-transferable and if the spouse can't go, then a relative or a friend can be invited to go instead.

NOTE: All the web addresses, URLs, and other contact details listed in this book were correct at press time. The Internet is very fluid and URLs, websites and web pages change daily. We will post all changes and updates on our website www.contestqueen.com.

WHY RUN A CONTEST?

No one runs a contest because they are feeling generous. Contests are a way for companies to attract or keep customers, pure and simple. They use our desire for the prize as a lure to get us to buy their products or expose ourselves to their advertising message. The advantage to the company is that the lure of the prize will keep customers' attention longer than other forms of advertising—we *want* what they are giving away, and are willing to endure their message or buy more of a product than we normally would to give ourselves a better chance of winning. Companies hold contests to:

- attract attention to their brand, product or service;
- increase sales;
- maintain or increase customer loyalty;
- increase their customer database;
- begin permission marketing. (You say it's OK for them to send you something via email or mail.)

A company needs to determine what it wants to accomplish and design a simple contest around that purpose.

If you ever feel a contest is confusing, complicated or unfair, contact the company promoting the contest (the management company, the sponsor or both) and ask for clarification of what you are finding frustrating. I have seen many contests change the entry page or the rules mid-promotion period, based on contestant feedback. Unfortunately, some companies make contests so complicated the original purpose of having the contest is defeated.

STORY: Susan submitted a good story on how some companies miss the point of a promotion (to create product or service awareness and attract new customers) by making the contest too confusing or difficult to enter.

₧)₨

Susan—Rose Bay, NS
A few months ago they had a contest in the local paper and you also had to listen to the local radio station for a daily clue letter. This went on for several weeks and my sister and I faithfully got each letter. They didn't have any letters for the weekends. If you didn't hear the letter, you could go to the local mall and the letters would be posted at the lotto booth. (It's 30 minute drive away for me.) You also had to cut four parts of a computer picture out of the local weekly paper (one each week for four weeks) and paste them on to the ballot. My other sister wanted to enter too, so she went to friends and got their old papers, since she and my mother share the paper. When the contest was over you had a week to put your entries in. It only took my sister and I a few hours to figure out the phrase, KNOWLEGE PAYS from the letters given. I took my mom's entry out with mine. My other two sisters took their ballots in separately. At the end of the contest my mom got a call that she had won the computer, printer, camera and scanner. When I went to take Mom to collect her prize, we ended up chatting with the girl in the lotto booth (where the letters were posted), and she said the contest must have been too complicated as there were only eight entries in the contest. Great odds!! Needless to say, my nephew (who lives with my mom most of the time) is in Grade 5 and it didn't take him long to hook up the computer. I wasn't there to see his eyes light up but I know he was thrilled to be able to do his homework on the computer. My mom, who is 70, still doesn't know much about it but wouldn't sell it and it's not hooked up to the Internet. What a wonderful win.

₧)₨

The premise of the promotion was to use multiple mass media vehicles and get people to participate. However, it was so difficult and cumbersome that most people were scared away or couldn't be bothered to enter resulting on only eight entries.

26

TIP: If a contest seems complicated, don't let it discourage you from entering. As Susan found, you might not have many other entries to compete against, which will increase your chances of winning.

Promotion Types

There is a difference between a lottery, a contest and a sweepstake even though in Canada we use the word contest interchangeably with the word sweepstake. It is important to understand the differences because it could determine what types of promotions you prefer to enter.

Lotteries and Sweepstakes Versus Contests

You're probably aware of the words "lotteries," "sweepstakes," and "contests," but you may not really understand how they differ from one another. This section will discuss their differences, as well and their relative advantages and disadvantages.

It's easier to define sweepstakes and contests by starting with their more familiar grandfather: the lottery. A lottery is any game that consists of three elements. These three elements are chance (luck), the entry fee (sometimes referred to as the "consideration"), and the prize. The first element—luck—is introduced by the very fact that you're competing against thousands of other people by predicting several numbers that will be chosen at random. The entry fee is generally the price of the ticket itself. Most lottery tickets cost one dollar. And the prizes are usually money.

What differentiates a sweepstakes or contest from a lottery is that one of these three elements has been removed. In a sweepstakes, that element is the entry fee. In other words, the game is still a game of chance, and there are still prizes to be won (although not necessarily cash prizes), but you don't have to pay to enter.

27

Contests retain the entry fee but remove the luck as a determining factor. The entry fee is usually in the form of purchasing one or more of the company's products. For example, a contest often requires you to send in a proof of purchase or label. Obviously, you cannot obtain these items without buying the product. It doesn't matter whether you personally bought it or one of your friends purchased it. The luck is removed by adding an element of skill. Whereas sweepstakes are determined through random drawings, contests require the participants to perform in some way. A contest may ask you to write a song or create a rhythm, or explain why you use a product. A panel of judges determines which contestant has demonstrated the most skill.

People tend to believe contests are more legitimate because they're sometimes required to pay an entry fee. One reason companies like contests so much is that they are another way of generating affordable advertising. Not only does the contest itself increase consumer interest, but the company might end up with a catchy slogan or jingle for its product when the contest is over. This slogan might just be as good as one created by a professional marketing firm, and the prize given to the winner is likely to be less expensive than hiring such a firm.

***How to Win Lotteries, Sweepstakes and Contests in the 21st Century* by Steve Ledoux. Copyright ©2004 Santa Monica Press LLC. Used by permission of Santa Monica Press LLC, 800-784-9553, www.santamonicapress.com.**

The laws that govern sweepstakes and contests in Canada are very simple. There are provisions in the Criminal Code and the Competition Act to ensure they are not "illegal lotteries". (see *Rules and Regulations*.) One of the provisions is the requirement for a No Purchase Entry (NPE). The NPE can be met by requiring a HDF (Hand

Drawn Facsimile) of a UPC (Universal Product Code) or have the contestant submit a short essay.

Purchase Requirement:

Section 206 of the *Criminal Code* prohibits purchase requirements for all "games of chance or mixed chance and skill" where the prizes consist of "goods, wares or merchandise". In all such cases, you must have a non-purchase means of entry. Usually, this is a hand-drawn facsimile of the entry form and/or of the UPC. You can also require a short (50-100 words) hand-written essay. Non-purchase entrants should be treated with "equal dignity": this means that you cannot require non-purchase entrants to inconvenience themselves in a major way or expend considerably more effort than "purchase" entrants. You *can* have a purchase requirement in two situations:

  a)   in a skill contest, *i.e.*, a contest where winners are determined solely on the basis of skill such as photography or writing contest; and
  b)   where *none* of the contest prizes fall into the category of "goods, wares or merchandise". Exempt prizes include cash, services (such as a car lease or a health club membership), trips and tickets to a concert or sporting event.

Reproduced with permission from LexisNexis Canada Inc., Pritchard & Vogt, Advertising and Marketing Law in Canada, 2004.

Lotteries

There are several different types of lotteries: jackpot draws (Super 7), sports games (Pro Line), daily draws (Pick 3), and instant games (Cash For Life) for example.

Information regarding each province's lotteries can be located at the following websites. The websites are quite comprehensive and have everything from winning numbers to Frequently Asked Questions regarding each lottery.

The Western Canada Lottery Corporation manages the lotteries for Alberta, Saskatchewan and Manitoba with the Yukon, Northwest Territories and Nunavut as associate members.
www.wclc.com

The British Columbia Lottery Corporation manages British Columbia.
www.bclc.com

The Atlantic Lottery Corporation manages the lotteries for New Brunswick, Nova Scotia, Prince Edward Island, Newfoundland and Labrador.
www.alc.ca

The Ontario Lottery and Gaming Corporation manages Ontario.
www.olgc.ca

Loto-Quebec manages Quebec.
www.loto-quebec.com

Lottery Canada is a national lottery portal.
www.lotterycanada.com

North American Association of State and Provincial Lotteries is an organization whose purpose is to be a hub of information for its members.
www.naspl.org

Sweepstakes

Most of this book is about sweepstakes, including the promotions I discuss, the methods of entry, and my Internet Contesting System. When I meet fellow contestors online or post to one of the contesting discussion groups, it is usually about a sweepstake. This is because sweepstakes, in general, require the least amount of effort to enter and can reap a great reward. You just need to fill out a ballot, submit it and hope you win. Most of the promotions I enter are sweepstakes. I enter a few contests and, on occasion, I buy lottery tickets.

Contests

There are all types of contests you can enter: cooking, baking, woodworking, writing and photography, to name just a few. These are great to enter because the number of entrants is usually quite low compared to sweepstakes (with the exception of the Annual Pillsbury Bake Off which garners hundreds of thousands of entries). So, if you have a particular hobby, skill or talent, look for contests where you can not only enjoy what you are doing (e.g. taking photographs or whittling wood) you can also possibly win cash and/or prizes.

Ironically, I rarely enter essay and story based contests. Let me explain. These types of contests are usually judged on the best story. I may write well, however, I feel I usually do not have a story good enough to win. I do enter many cooking and baking contests because cooking and baking are another love of mine. For example, my chili recipe won 3rd prize in a Super Bowl of Chili Cook Off in 2002.

Carolyn's Award-Winning Awesome Chicken Chili

3lbs. ground chicken (I prefer to grind my own using skinless boneless thighs.)
1 large spanish onion, diced
1 tbsp. olive oil
4 large or 6 medium tomatoes, diced (a can of diced tomatoes can be used if desired)
1 green pepper, seeded and diced
1 red pepper, seeded and diced
1 yellow pepper, seeded and diced
1 orange pepper, seeded and diced
1 cubanelle pepper, seeded and diced
1 hot banana pepper, seeded and diced
1 jalapeno pepper, seeded and diced
1 chili pepper, seeded and finely diced (use gloves for this step, trust me!)
1 tbsp. chili powder*
1 tbsp. hot chili flakes*
10 dashes of Tabasco
1 tsp. salt*
1 tsp. ground black pepper*

31

1 19oz. can black beans, drained and rinsed
1 19oz. can kidney beans, drained and rinsed

This is one of the easiest recipes ever. I place all the
ingredients (except for the oil, the onion and the
chicken) in to an 8qt. pot and turn the heat on low. In
a cold frying pan pour in the oil and turn the heat on
medium low (the cooking temperatures were
determined by my halogen stove top and may be
adjusted for your stove). Once the oil is hot, turn the
heat to low, put the onion in the pan, sauté until soft,
and then add the onion to the pot. In the same frying
pan, place the raw chicken (add a bit more oil if it is
required) and cook until there is no pink colour left.
(I find the chicken browns faster if I put the lid on the
frying pan.) Drain the chicken and then add the
chicken to the pot. Stir about every ½ hour. Put the
lid on until the chili boils then I find the chili turns
out best if cooked on low without a lid for 3-4 hours.
Otherwise, there is too much liquid and it is too
runny to scoop with chips.
*to taste

My prize for such a delicious recipe was a nice basket of Tabasco
branded goodies including an apron, a golf shirt, a silk scarf and
enough Tabasco sauce to make a ton of chili!

I also collect cook books and my father purchased an old box at an
auction. In the box was *The Nellie Aldridge Cook Book—Many Ways to
Utilize the Citrus Fruits of the San Bernardo Valley*. The book is
undated. Inside is a wonderful example of a contest entry from days
gone-by.

Orange Sunshine Cake
Whites of 10 eggs, yolks of 6 eggs; 1 cup granulated
sugar, 1 teaspoon flavoring, 1 cup Swan's Down cake
Flour, 1 teaspoon cream of tartar. Beat whites of eggs
until stiff and dry, add sugar gradually and continue
beating; then add yolks of eggs beaten until thick and

lemon colored, and 1 teaspoon orange extract. Cut and fold in flour mixed and sifted with cream of tartar. Bake 60 minutes in a slow oven*, in an angel cake pan.

In a cake baking contest held by Misses Hancock and Wade of the Home Furniture Company of San Bernardino this cake scored 98½ points winning a $55.00 Acorn Gas Range, given as a prize for the best cake.
*A slow oven is 300°F.

NOTE: There is a difference between a contest that wants you to submit a story (e.g. why your mom is the best) and a sweepstake's no purchase entry option asking you to submit your entry along with a 100-word essay. The contest winner will be selected by a panel of judges and the sweepstake winner will be drawn at random. Therefore, even if you feel you don't not have the best creative writing skills, and wouldn't enter the contest, enter the sweepstake as your writing skills will not be judged.

*"Anybody can win unless there
happens to be a second entry."*
George Ade

RULES AND REGULATIONS

My #1 tip:
<u>READ THE RULES *AND* FOLLOW THEM!!</u>

This is my number one tip because most people don't read the rules.
One company I interviewed said only 2% of the people clicked the
Rules and Regulation button on online contest entry pages. Another
source stated that up to 40% of mail-in entries were disqualified
because the rules were not followed.

It is <u>very important</u> to read the rules and regulations to see:
- if you are eligible to enter.
- how many times you can enter.
- how many people in the household can enter.
- the start and end dates of the contest.
- any other rules specific to that contest.

I have potentially disqualified myself countless times by not reading
the rules before I enter. I have entered:
- out-of-province or out-of-country contests.
- more than once in a one-entry-per-person contest.
- both my husband and myself in one-entry-per-household contest.
- before the contest starts.
- my husband in women only contests.
- contests where I did not meet the age requirements.

Many contests have overlapping methods of entry. Reading the rules
will also allow you to determine the best entry method for you.

Brenda Pritchard and Susan Vogt of Gowling Lafleur Henderson (www.gowlings.com) are two of Canada's leading advertising and marketing lawyers. (Contesting law falls within this specialty.) Their book, *Advertising and Marketing Law in Canada*, is a must read for all advertising and marketing professionals. They give a good overview of who is responsible for the rules in Canada, especially Quebec.

The Ground Rules:

Every contest and incentive program is a contract between the promoter and participants. The terms of the contract are set out in either the contest rules or the terms and conditions of the offer. Most advertisers wouldn't sign a business contract without careful attention to the legal side, but many people in marketing do not realize the legal implications of the contracts they regularly extend to consumers in the form of contests and premium offers.

Contest rules must be comprehensive, unambiguous and clearly communicated to consumers. The same applies to the terms and conditions of other incentive programs. If these contracts are incomplete or poorly drafted and you have to rely on them in court, be aware of the legal rule of *contra preferendum*. Any ambiguity in a contract is interpreted against the party who drafted the contract: in this case, the promoter or advertiser.

To assist in understanding the potential issues and weeding through the legal boilerplate, there are draft contest rules set later in this chapter. In a good set of rules or terms and conditions, every word is there for a reason.

Equally important is the applicable legislation. Promotional contests are governed by the *Competition Act*, the *Criminal Code* and Quebec's *Act respecting lotteries alcohol, publicity contests and amusement machines*.

Before discussing the law, we will briefly define some terms. Contests can be divided into two broad categories: skill contests and contests where prizes are awarded at random. Skill contests—where winners are selected by experienced judges based on the contestants' skill at story-writing, photography, *etc.*—are rare. Much more common, in fact ubiquitous, are contests where winners are randomly selected.

These include sweepstakes—where prizes are awarded by random draw; seeded games (including Coke's "under the bottle cap" promotions and Tim Hortons's "Roll Up the Rim to Win") where prizes are randomly seeded on game cards or on-pack and participants must scratch, unpeel or otherwise reveal the prize area to discover whether they have won a prize; "match and win" games where participants must collect game pieces to spell specific words or match the pieces of a puzzle. "Match and win" games are usually structured to include "rare pieces" which make the odds of winning a major prize astronomical. There are as many varieties of random contests as imaginative marketers can devise.

Quebec—Régie des alcools des courses et des jeux
Whether or not to include Quebec residents in a contest is often determined by whether you want to deal with the Régie. The Régie has jurisdiction over all contests which are "launched to the public" in Quebec. Thus, employee contests are not governed by the Régie but trade promotions are. In most cases, the Régie does not have jurisdiction over skill contests. All "public contests" which are open to Quebec residents must be registered with the Régie unless the total prize value is less than $2,000. You should note however, that if the prize pool is less than $2,000 but more than $100, the "duty" will still have to be paid to the Régie.

Complete information on registering your contest
with the Régie is available at www.racj.gouv.qc.ca. If
you need to deal with the Régie, you should consider
the following:

a) Who should file the registration documents?
   If anyone other than the sponsor or the
   sponsor's lawyer registers the contest, they
   will have to file a proxy.

b) Contest rules and contest-related advertising
   must be filed with the Régie 10 days before
   the start date. These should be filed in
   French unless the contest will be carried
   only in English media.

c) The Régie assesses taxes at the rate of 3 per
   cent of total prize value for a national
   contest or 10 per cent of the value of prizes
   allocated to Quebec residents. If the contest
   is a scratch and win or otherwise seeded,
   you only have to pay taxes on the value of
   the prizes you estimate will be redeemed.
   Taxes and the registration documents are
   due 30 days before the contest start date.
   The usual penalty for late filing is interest on
   the late payment of taxes.

d) If the value of any prize offered to Quebec
   residents exceeds $5,000 or the total prizes
   offered to Quebec residents exceeds
   $20,000, you will have to file a security
   bond.

e) Within 60 days of the contest's draw date,
   you have to file a final report (*i.e.*, a
   winners' list) with the Régie.

f) You cannot amend or withdraw a contest in
   Quebec without the Régie's approval.

g) The Régie requires you to keep all contest
   entry forms for 120 days following the draw
   date.

h) If a contest falls within the Régie's
   jurisdiction, the rules and advertising must

38

include specific clauses that are not required
in the rest of Canada. These are set out in
sections 5 and 6 of "Rules respecting
publicity contests."

**Reproduced with permission from LexisNexis
Canada Inc., Pritchard & Vogt, Advertising and
Marketing Law in Canada, 2004.**

I Didn't Read the Rules

I received a very exciting email one day informing me I had won a trip
to Santa Fe and Taos, New Mexico. Then I read the fine print: I had
only won the hotel stay. Airfare and car rental were not included. What
was I thinking?! Why would I enter a contest that wasn't all inclusive??
Apparently, I had not read the rules very carefully. I looked up the
hotels on the Internet. They looked very nice. The hotel stay was worth
quite a bit. Hmmm…what to do, what to do?! I talked it over with my
husband and we decided to go. Luckily for us we had airline points
saved up so we cashed them in for the airfare and part of the car rental.
New Mexico was not a holiday destination I would normally think of.
We had a great time and I highly recommend going if you are looking
for somewhere new to visit. The landscape was gorgeous, the food was
fantastic and the people were wonderful. Craig and I would like to go
back.

Since we had enough
points saved to cover
airfare and car rentals,
this story had a happy
ending. It could have
cost us a pretty penny or
I may have had to turn
down the prize. You can
be sure that now, I
always read the rules
thoroughly. Sometimes
I even read them twice!

I will repeat my #1 contesting tip because it is so important:
<u>READ THE RULES *AND* FOLLOW THEM!!</u>

"Luck is believing you're lucky."
Tennessee Williams

FIVE WAYS TO ENTER

There are five ways a company will promote a contest:

- in-store
- radio/call-in
- mail-in
- internet
- text messaging (cell phone)

In-Store

In-store contests are either a fill-in ballot type sweepstake, a game piece collection style promotion or a seeded contest.

The ballot style of promotion is designed to draw in foot traffic and potential sales into the store or near the product sponsoring the promotion, as well as to expand the store's mailing list. They are usually found at the front of the store or near the cash register. The odds in this type of promotion are usually good since many times the prize is one per store, the entry period is short, it has not been advertised to the general public and the people that do enter, generally only fill out one ballot.

TIP: Do not swipe the entire entry pad, fill the ballots out at home and return them to the store. The contest may have unlimited entries, however it is on the edge of cheating and it is not good karma. (see Attracting Luck.)

If the rules are available, it is important to read them. If the ballot style draw is being held by a major retail chain, the rules are usually printed on the back of the ballot or posted near the ballot box. Major retailers have been known to limit draws to one entry per person or one entry per household for the entire chain. They also do not necessarily pool all

41

the ballots together. I have seen promotions where the ballots are filled out country wide, and then a particular store is chosen; a name is then selected from the ballot box in that specific store. Another method is a few ballots from each store are sent to the company's head office, and the winner is selected from those ballots only.

Game sweepstakes originally were only conducted with the in-store method of entry. With the advent of Internet sweepstakes, some game sweepstakes now involve purchasing or mailing away for PIN codes (Personal Identification Number) or games pieces to be entered on a specific online contest website.

NOTE: PIN code based contests are being run more frequently by sponsor companies because it makes it easy for the average consumer to enter once while at the same time making it harder for a contestor to enter multiple times.

Game sweepstakes are the fastest growing form of sweepstakes today. The major reason for their popularity is that a sweepstakes player participates in finding out whether or not he or she has won a prize.

Some sweepstakes players view game sweepstakes as the fast food version of "regular" sweepstakes—they remove some of the mystery from sweepstakes. In random draw sweepstakes, one fills out and submits an entry, not certain whether the entry will win or lose. Players are only notified later if they win. There is no way to know whether you have lost a sweepstakes unless you request a winners list. (We've never heard of a judging organization that notifies the losers.)

In game sweepstakes, the number of prizes and the number of entries are predetermined. The number of entries is determined by the number of game pieces printed. (Only a fixed percentage of the total number of game pieces printed are winners.) The number of people playing a game sweepstakes has no effect on your chances of winning. Either you get a winning card or you do not.

Not all game sweepstakes are the same. There are five types of game sweepstakes: collect, match, decode and instant-win predetermined and instant-win probability.

Collect. To win the collect game sweepstakes, the entrant must collect game pieces (of which usually one is rare) to spell a word, build a picture, and so forth. Many potential players unwittingly discard the rare piece.

Match. Match game sweepstakes usually involve matching a number or picture from a game piece to a list of winning selections. Typically, the winning selections are posted in retail stores, or can be obtained through the mail.

Decode. Decode game sweepstakes usually instruct the entrant to take his or her game piece to a special decoding display in a store to see if it is a winner. The game pieces are always scrambled so that it cannot be read without the "special" decoder. Some new fangled decode sweepstakes require computer equipment to play. In 1989 K Mart put bar codes on store flyers which customers brought to K Mart stores to be scanned. The computer announced if and what the customer won.

Instant-Win Predetermined. Predetermined instant-win sweepstakes usually feature a game piece from which you scratch off a covering layer, which reveals any prize that may have been won. For example, in scratching a card three panels may be revealed; if all match, the card is a winner. How you scratch the game piece has no affect because the outcome is predetermined.

43

It is sometimes possible to differentiate winning and losing game pieces prior to playing if the pieces were printed separately. One can look for slight differences such as a filled in letter "e" or a stray dot that might appear only on winning game pieces.

Instant-Win Probability. In probability games, every piece is a potential winner if scratched or played properly. For example, Applian Way Pizza ran a probability instant-win game in which ten spots were covered with a film layer. Two of the ten spots carried matching prizes. If they player could uncover the matching spots with only two scratches, he or she won the prize indicated. Every game card was a potential winner of $5 to $5,000.

**Copyright ©1990 by Jeffrey & Robin Sklar.
Extract from *Winning Sweepstakes* published by
Sebell Publishing Company Inc.**

Seeded contests are the hardest to win because it involves finding the winning piece in thousands or even millions of product containers (e.g. bottle cap liners, toilet rolls, talking cans, etc.). Charlie and the Chocolate Factory (by Ronald Dahl) is a fictional example of a seeded contest. The children had to be lucky enough to find a golden ticket in the chocolate bar packaging to win an invitation to the chocolate factory.

Most promotions have a NPE (No Purchase Entry) option where you can send away for a free package sample, PIN code, entry form, etc. Legally, the odds are the same if you bought the product or send away for a NPE.

NOTE: There is a difference between collect-to-win and seeded contests even though both have very rare winning pieces, coupons, notifications, etc. In the collect-to-win you get a game piece(s) with every purchase and you hope you get one of the rare winning pieces. In seeded contests you do not collect anything. You just hope you are lucky enough to find the winning certificate, notification, etc.

Radio/Phone In

Radio contests are designed to keep a listener hooked for their next opportunity to call in and win. When larger prizes are given away, they are designed to keep listeners hooked for days or weeks at a time. You will generally find the larger the market, the better the prizes. This is because in larger cities, they have more listeners; therefore they can charge their advertisers more and have more funds available for bigger promotions. It is usually also more difficult to "get through" on the contest line as more people are trying to qualify or win the giveaway.

NOTE: You can listen to many radio stations from around the globe online. Be aware: 1) there is usually minor time delay between what is aired live on the radio and what is aired over the Internet and 2) many radio stations require you to pick-up your prize in person at the station. If you live in Vancouver, you may enjoy the music from the Halifax radio station but you may be wasting your time trying to win their promotions.

The first contest I can remember entering was a radio contest to see Burton Cummings at Hamilton Place. I stood in the kitchen for ages dialing on a rotary dial phone hoping to be the fourth caller through. I was so excited when I won those tickets. I was only fourteen so my mom had to go down and pick up the tickets. She also went with me to the concert. We sat fourth row center. I felt so grown-up and so lucky!

With life getting busier and busier, I find I am rarely entering radio call-in contests. I always seem to be driving or on a call when the announcer plays the cue to call in. I know there are many people who have tremendous luck calling-in-to-win. Try this method of contesting and decide for yourself if it is for you.

TIP: Bea had a really good tip on how she "gets through" on her local radio station's contest line. She won a trip to see U2 in Los Angeles.

ಬಿಂಬ

Bea—Toronto, ON
The redial button on the phone that I qualified on is really fast. I have a cordless phone and another phone that is more expensive but slow in redialing. The main suggestion I have is before you hear the cue to call

45

is to start calling. With this contest I had to call after hearing two U2 songs. In between they placed the cue but I literally started a couple seconds before. Never give up. I know that radio call in contests can be more difficult but be persistent. I was going to give up since I didn't qualify the first weekend. I could hardly believe it when the DJs called me Monday morning to tell me I had won. I had forgotten to set my alarm and literally woke up seconds before the phone rang. We had an awesome time at the concert.

∞⋆⋆

TIP: To increase your odds of dialing in and getting through, try listening to less popular radio stations.

I did have great luck with one call-in-to-win contest. When my daughter was an infant I was able to call in to qualify my husband for a "Guy's Get-Away". I think it was at the height of my contesting obsession. It was 7:00am on a Sunday morning. I was breast feeding my daughter in front of the computer while I entered contests online. In the background I had the radio on listening for my cue to call in. When I heard the signal, I dialed right away. I was caller one. I thought, "Darn, I dialed too fast." Then I thought, "I should try again." I was caller two. I looked at the phone puzzled. I called back. I was callers three, four, five and six! I don't think anyone else was listening at that hour. I knew then we were going to win. Since it was a male oriented prize I gave the announcer my husband's name.

The next morning was the big draw. I was up at 5:00am feeding my daughter and heard which DJ was announcing that morning. Then I went back to bed turning the ringer on our phone back on. (It had been turned off since our daughter had been born.) At 7:10am the phone rang. I picked it up and sure enough it was the DJ. I screamed "WE WON! WE WON!" shaking awake my sound asleep husband. He sat up bewildered and I handed

him the phone. They confirmed it was him and told him he was going to Florida to be a judge in the Miss Hawaiian Tropics Bikini Contest State Finals. We had a ball. I don't think we could have fit anymore fun into three days. All his friends wanted to know where they could find a wife like me (or like the bikini models!).

Mail-in

The topic of mail-in (aka snail mail) contesting is vast. This section could be a book in itself. I do not plan to rewrite what many others have already written on the topic. There are many good books on the market today focusing on mail-in contests and a few of my preferred books are listed in the Recommended Reading section of this book. I will skim the topic to give you an overview.

Mail-in contests can be found in many places including retail stores, magazines, newspapers, and online (some contests have PDF ballots that you can download and print off at home). Mail-in contests and sweepstakes in Canada are getting harder to find as companies move towards online based promotions. This is a straight bottom line decision: it is far less expensive to run an online promotion than a mail based promotion. The upside for contestors is there are fewer people entering mail-in contests, so the odds are getting better for those that do. The easiest way to find mail-in contests is to subscribe to one or more of the newsletters listed in this section.

There are many different ways a mail-in promotion can be run. Some ask for an Official Entry Form, a PPP (Plain Piece of Paper) or a postcard. You may be asked for a UPC (Universal Product Code) or a HDF (Hand Drawn Facsimile). There is a trend right now leaning away from UPCs and towards a short essay being submitted in lieu of a product purchase.

NOTE: If a contest has both a mail-in and Internet entry option, use the Internet option. Many companies treat mail-in entries like Internet entries by either coding them or opening the envelope and typing the information into the computer system. You are wasting time and money mailing into these types of promotions. I recommend always entering via the Internet. It is only beneficial if the rules state one online entry and unlimited mail-in entries.

Like all contests, it's always important to read the rules so you know how many in the household can enter, how often you can enter, the contest end date, how they would like the ballot sent in and if there is a No Purchase Entry option. This will determine your contest entry method(s). My personal favourites are one entry per person or one entry per household contests because: 1) everyone has an equal chance to win and 2) they take far less time to enter.

Staggering & Flooding

Staggering is the method of submitting entries "staggered" over the entire contest entry period. Flooding is the method of sending so many entries you have "flooded" the ballot box, drawing drum or online database.

Due to the drawing methods of mail-in promotions it is a good idea to stagger your entries throughout the entire contest period. Due to the volume of mail most contests receive, it is impossible to put all the envelopes into the drawing drum and select the winner(s). Most contest management companies either: 1) select a few entries from each mailbag and put those in the drum or 2) they open the envelope and enter your data into a computerized database for that sweepstake. Mailing in entries over the entire contest period increases the chances your entry will be in the drawing drum. (see *Increasing Your Chances*.)

When you "flood" a contest, you are basically trying to increase the odds of having the winning entry form. Try this. Take a dice and throw it. The dice has six sides and the "odds" of you throwing a "one" is one in six. You may however throw the dice one hundred times and never have the "one" land face up. Each time you throw the dice the odds are still one in six. Now take a quarter or dime and throw it. You win if the coin lands face-up. The odds of this happening are one-in-two. Try throwing a coin a number of times and count how many times you get the face-up. You could throw the coin one hundred times and never have it land face-up, on the other hand it could land face-up each and every time. The odds are still one-in-two.

48

By flooding a contest you are increasing your chances of winning. That is a reality. However, even if you manage to have enough entries in the contest to be working with one-in-two odds, you may still not win.

Some people "flood" a contest and then get really upset when they don't win. They figure the judges are cheating or that they are blacklisted. If it is a nationally run contest, the more likely reality is that they just didn't get picked. On some of the local and in-store draw contests, they could be right, in which case you can increase your odds of winning by putting in fewer entries!

Extract from Winning Ways by Lynn Banks Goutbeck and Melanie Rockett. Used by permission of Proof Positive Productions Ltd. www.proofpositive.com.

Lingo

Abbreviations are generally associated with mail-in contests but have sometimes been found in the rules of Internet contests. These are a few of the most common abbreviations you will come across while contesting:

FR—Form Required
HDF—Hand Drawn Facsimile
NAP—Name Address Phone Number
NAPA—Name Address Phone Number Age
NPE—No Purchase Entry
PPP—Plain Piece of Paper
SASE—Self Addressed Stamped Envelope
SMP—Specially Marked Package
STQ—Skill Testing Question
UPC—Universal Product Code

TIP: If a contest asks for an essay with a specific word count (e.g. 500-word essay) type it out on your PC first, using a program like Word,

*and using the WORD COUNT feature to get the precise word count.
Then depending on the rules, you can either print it out and submit it or
copy out by hand what you have just typed.*

Postal Standards

Canada Post has set-out envelope and postcard addressing standards
(along with other standards) that should be followed to ensure your
mail-in entries are delivered properly. This is especially important if
you choose to decorate, embellish or create your own envelopes. Size,
weight and other factors may affect the amount of postage required or
the mailability of your item.

You should visit the Canada Post website at:
www.canadapost.ca/tools/pg/default-e.asp and follow the addressing
format and location guidelines and other requirements. Check back
periodically as postal standards can and do change.

*TIP: Key search words to use on the Canada Post website include:
address format; lettermail; non-mailable and envelopes.*

Envelopes

I purposely put Canada's postal standards before this section on
envelopes. Decorated, embellished and handmade envelopes are very
popular amongst snail mail contestors. Most of the contesting books I
have read all recommend mailing in envelopes "that stand out" to
increase the odds of winning. The authors (and many fellow contestors)
feel they win more using these types of envelopes. I think the reason
many contestors believe they win with decorated, embellished and
handmade envelopes is because they are using The Law of Attraction
(see *Attracting Luck.*). They are putting their winning thoughts and
energies into and onto the envelope and sending it off into the universe
(via Canada Post). This in turn sub-consciously attracts the person
selecting the winner to that particular entry.

I have experimented using both types of envelopes. I have not found a
difference in sending in plain envelopes vs. decorated ones. I currently
send in plain envelopes. It is less time consuming to create and costs
less money since I am not purchasing markers, stickers, glue, etc...

Lynn Goutbeck (co-author of *Winning Ways*) loved to decorate and embellish her envelopes. She even sent me a package once with examples of her envelopes because she was so excited about her cute designs. She saved money on envelopes by using all the ones that came in the mail with bills. Since they would be decorated, it didn't matter if they were plain or had writing and corporate logos on them. Lynn would purchase inexpensive used children's books and packs of used birthday cards, Christmas cards and postcards. She would cut the book pages and the cards to fit the envelope, glue pictures on the front and back, ensuring the flap would close properly, and put plain white labels where the return and mail-to addresses should go. She swore her designs were the source of her good fortune. I believed her.

NOTE: If you choose to make your own envelopes, check the Canada Post website regarding postal standards to ensure your envelopes will be mailable.

I also met a woman (who asked to remain anonymous) who, in the last 10 years, has won 11 cars, over 100 trips and thousands of prizes. She sends in the plainest, simplest envelopes she can. She feels the contest management companies and judging agencies prefer to give away prizes to an average consumer rather than a "professional" contestor. She said that the coloured and embellished envelopes are a dead give-away to the companies that it was sent in by a contestor and her plain envelopes allow her to blend in with the average contestants. I cannot argue with her winning track record.

Try both methods and decide for yourself which one works better for you.

NOTE: If you choose to decorate or embellish your envelopes, ensure you adhere to Canada Post's standards and do not draw, colour, paint, glue or place stickers within the areas that are to remain clear. This will help ensure your entry is delivered properly. Also, keep all embellishments flat and do not use raised or puffy stickers, glue, paint etc. as they could catch in the postal machines ruining your contest entry.

TIP: Use a standard #10 for your mail-in entries. Many companies I interviewed said if the envelope is too large, it will not fit into the drawing drum. The entry would then either be removed and placed into a smaller envelope or discarded altogether.

Postcards

Many contests ask you to send in your entry on a postcard. I do not pay for the postcards I use for contesting. I get my postcards free from various Toronto shops and restaurants. I even grabbed a few every time I saw some in Europe, (on a trip we won) hoping some of the winning mojo would continue onto the next contest. (see *Attracting Luck*.)

NOTE: Go to Zoom Media Inc (www.zoom-media.com/en/index _flash.cfm) and select POSTCARDS to see an example of the type of display you should be looking for to obtain free postcards.

TIP: To prevent postcards entries from accidentally being returned back to you by the post office, write FROM and TO above each address and highlight the entire TO address.

TIP FROM LOIS: Turn the postcard vertically and write the FROM information perpendicular to the TO information. I do this because a friend of mine was a postal employee and told me the machines send the card to whichever address they "read" first. If the FROM address is sideways it will not be read.

A standard postcard is 4¼" x 6". If a contest asks for a 3"x5" postcard, you can cut a regular postcard down and place it in an envelope. I do this because they are too small to mail.

As long as the rules do not specifically state the required postcard's dimensions, another option is to use shaped postcards, although additional postage may apply. These are usually sold along side regular postcards. They are a bit more expensive, however the card's surface area is generally much larger than a standard postcard and the varied sides could provide a better opportunity to be selected.

NOTE: Check with your local post office as the shaped postcards may require additional postage.

STORY: Erin sent me the story of her favourite mail-in entry win. She nearly didn't get notified.

శోస్త

Erin—Riverview, NB

One of my biggest wins was through a mail-in contest. The contest was sponsored by Butler Gum and they were giving away several trips for two to an all-inclusive Sandals resort in Jamaica. I believe one trip was to be drawn for Atlantic Canada, one for Ontario, one for Quebec and one for Western Canada. I only entered the contest twice, but I ended up being the winner for Atlantic Canada! I was notified by mail. I received an envelope that wasn't even sealed. I pulled out the papers and apologized to my sister for winning a trip to where she wanted to go. I have actually won a trip every year for the past three years. Can't wait to find out where I am going next.

శోస్త

Universal Product Codes & Hand Drawn Facsimiles

Hand Drawn Facsimiles (HDF) are great topic of discussion between fellow contestors. Each of us seems to have our own method of creating them.

 I use a 3" x 5" card cut in half. I turn it sideways and use a skinny black marker and a fat black marker to create the lines. I then carefully print in the numbers. My HDFs are not very neat. I free hand the lines. I do ensure all twelve numbers are on the HDF and are legible. The Universal Product Code (UPC) numbers are what they verify if your entry is selected. I have won mail-in contests using my method so I know neatness does not always count.

STORY: Lois is very "old school". She has been contesting for over 25 years so most of her contest system and experience came long before the Internet.

ജ൬

Lois—Lowbanks, ON
Since I have been contesting for so long I am in the habit of keeping every UPC from everything I buy. Sometimes it comes in very handy. One time when a new contest started I already had over thirty UPCs in my file folder and could enter right away. I didn't even have to make any HDFs.

Many times though I do not have as many UPCs on hand as entries I would like to send in. I have created a real time saving method. I take an 8½" x 11" sheet of paper. I turn it sideways and using a ruler and various sized pens, I create eighteen UPCs (six across and three up). I try to make mine look as close to the original UPC as I can. It only takes me 15 minutes to create an entire sheet.

ജ൬

NOTE: For those sending in original UPCs from wet or moist food products for a contest, please <u>wash</u> the UPC first because otherwise the entries can get quite smelly.

TIP: If you do not have a UPC handy to enter, you can look up UPCs on the Internet and use the numbers to create HDFs. Many of the online groups have UPC databases or you can look here: www.somewhereincanada.com/upc/ (NOTE: UPCs are different in Canada then they are in the US. Ensure you are using Canadian UPCs.)

Craig and I had a GREAT win via mail. It was a promotion being held by a very popular fabric softener company. They had sent a sample to our house to try a new scent. Along with the sample was a mail-in ballot to win a washer and dryer or a few other prizes. It was a one entry per household contest.

One day our mailperson came to the door with a registered letter. I had won first prize: a $2000 Roots gift certificate!! I needed a new winter coat, and had never owned a leather jacket… and besides, a girl can never have too many purses!

It was mid-December when we won. I knew if I mailed the release forms back in the enclosed envelope they could get lost or delayed in the Christmas mail. I chose to spend the money and couriered the release forms back. That was a wise decision for two reasons: 1) I knew it got there and 2) they were able to send my gift certificates back to me right away. My husband and I were able to buy far more than we normally would have because of the great Boxing Day sales.

What I found ironic was on the ballot they had asked my opinion on the new scent and I told them the truth. I did not like it, I thought it smelled like bubble gum and I would not buy this particular scent, ever! I still won and I do buy their original scent.

Newsletters

NOTE: All the newsletters listed are paid subscription publications. The prices were correct at the time of printing and are subject to change.

Canadian Contests

www.canadiancontests.com
The newsletter Canadian Contests was started by Sherry Blakelock in 1990 and featured all types of mail-in contests. Lori Novak purchased the business from Amy, Sherry's daughter in 2003. The newsletter publishes ten times per year and is mailed out monthly (with the exception of February and August). Since the advent of the Internet, coverage is now split approximately 50/50 between mail-in contests and Internet contests. Subscribers have the option of receiving the newsletter in PDF format via email or a printed copy via the mail. The website is a portal to information about the newsletter, sample contests and a subscription form. The annual subscription fee is $31.00

Contest Canada

www.contestcanada.com/snailmail
This newsletter was started in 2002 by Joe Head as an extension of the contests listed on his website www.contestcanada.com. The newsletter only features Canadian contests that can be entered via regular mail. It was originally sent out via email to all its subscribers and is now

accessed online. There is a $25.00 annual fee for access to this web-based newsletter.

Trader's Forum & Win A Contest

www.somewhereincanada.com/tf

www.winacontest.com

Sylvia Gold started Trader's Forum in 1996. It is a cornucopia of anything manufacturers have to offer; coupons, rebates, bonus offers, contests, etc. and is mailed out once per month. Sample copies are available for $5.00, $21.00 for a six month subscription and $36.00 for an annual subscription.

Norman Holt started Win A Contest in 1997. It is sent out via email and regular mail. Sylvia was one of the first subscribers. In 2003 Norman became too ill to continue managing the newsletter, and Sylvia offered to take over. Unlike Traders Forum, it focuses only on contests. A mailed subscription is sent out every two weeks. It is $42.00 for an annual subscription ($45.00 for Ontario) and the emailed version is sent out every week. It is $20.00 for an annual subscription ($21.60 for Ontario). Please make all cheques payable to S. Gold.

Internet

My favourite way to enter sweepstakes is via the Internet. It's fast, free, and there are more and more promotions online every day. The downside is, since it is so quick and easy to enter, more and more people have picked up Internet contesting as a hobby. This means more competition, which affects the odds of winning.

The main focus of this book is on the fast growing method of Internet contesting. I will discuss the many ways you can use the Internet to enhance your hobby, including websites that feature portals to newsletters, forums where you can meet like minded people online, sites that host online promotions, and methods of protecting yourself from hackers and con artists.

Websites

There are many Canadian websites that either post contests online directly or offer a link to a newsletter subscription.

NOTE: ✉ = *free e-newsletter offered on website.*

About Contests ✉
http://contests.about.com
Tom Stamatson and his wife Ingrid have been entering and writing about contests for over 25+ years. Even though Tom is located in Wichita, Kansas, I have included this resource because his information is very useful for contestors everywhere. There are quite a few contest resources, the How-To articles being my favorite. Click on STAY-UP-TO-DATE to sign-up for his free e-newsletter and three contest lessons (via email). There is also a forum—however, since this is a US-based site, the interaction between fellow "sweepers" will probably not be relevant to Canadians.

TIP: Ensure whenever you sign up for emails coming from a major website you set your spam filters to accept emails from that organization (e.g. Contest Guide & about.com).

Canada Contests ✉
www.canadacontests.com
Tony Sylvain owns All About Websites (www.allaboutwebsites.com) and launched Canada Contests in 1999 as a marketing tool for his clients. Membership is required and is free. Members receive a new contest to their inbox daily. Members can post new contests by uploading the promotion information.

TIP: Keep a small notebook by your computer to write notes, codes and UPCs for current contest and future reference.

Canadiannetstakes ✉
www.canadiannetstakes.com
Canadiannetstakes is owned and operated by Promodem Media Inc. They post all the contests they manage for their clients on this site. Promodem's contests tend to be fun. For example, many not only have a standard entry feature, they also have games that, if played, garner the contestant bonus entries. Sign-up for their e-newsletter and receive announcements as to when new contests are posted.

Canuck Cash ✉

www.canuckcash.ca

Dave Rossborough started contesting in much the same way I did. He had a hiatus between projects and discovered the world of "sweeping" and contestors. After his first win, he was hooked! He started Canuck Cash in 2001 as a very simple site to promote Canadian contests and it has grown from there. You must become a member to use the site. Membership is free and gives members exclusive access to post their own contests, join the community, and receive the latest Canadian contest information. Once you join, you automatically get the daily e-newsletter, which is a collection of all the freebies and contests posted that day.

Concours Exchangeboard ✉

http://concours.exchangeboard.com

NOTE: This site is in French.

In 1999 Dominique Belisle started Concours Exchangeboard. In 2004 the site was revamped to better meet the needs of Quebec contestors. They are currently building a Membership section which will include such features as contest answers and UPC codes (when required), more detailed descriptions, less advertising, etc. An e-newsletter called HEBDO-CONCOURS is sent out twice monthly. An English version of the site is planned for the near future.

Concoursweb ✉

www.concoursweb.com

NOTE: This site is in French.

Sacha Sylvain began entering contests because a close friend of his and her mother were contestors and winning on a regular basis. Being an avid "techie" and contestor, he created the Concoursweb site in 2002 because contests were not easy to find on the Internet and even more so in Quebec. The site is updated daily with new contests and promotions. You can also sign-up for his free e-newsletter.

Contest Canada

www.contestcanada.com

This site was originally started by Joe Head as ww2.sympatico.ca/contest. He teamed up with David Larade in 2000, and Contest Canada was born. The contests posted on this site are open only to Canadians. Some contests are province or city specific. Sign up for the free membership because once you join, the site offers members a great bookmarking feature. It allows you to track contests in a similar manner to my Internet contesting system. The website does not host a forum. To fill the void, Joe moderates I Can Win, http://groups.yahoo.com/group/icanwin. (see *Join an Online Community*.)

ContestGuru ⊠

www.contestguru.com
Contest Guru is owned by Melanie Rockett. You may recognize her as the co-author (with Lynn Goutbeck) of "Winning Ways," a top-selling contesting book in the early 90's. Melanie has a new e-book called "Contest Guru's Guide to Winning Sweepstakes." It is available on her website free of charge.

In addition to being a sweepstakes enthusiast, Melanie is also interested in skill-based contests. Seven years ago she launched www.proofpositive.com as a way of helping and mentoring other freelance writers and photographers. She encourages freelancers to enter skill-based contests as a self-promotion strategy. The contesting portion of her site became so popular that she spun it off to a new website www.contestguru.com. ContestGuru has hundreds of skill-based contests for writers, poets, photographers, song writers and cooks as well as contests that focus on short essays, slogans and jingles.

You can sign-up on her site for free membership, which allows you to post new contests, report broken links, etc. Send a blank email to contest_news@getresponse.com to sign-up for her free e-newsletter.

Contest Hound ⊠

www.contesthound.ca
Bob Gunther started Contest Hound in 1999 after his first daughter was born and he decided to be a stay-at-home dad. Originally, all the Canadian contests we listed under their own heading on the .com site and the .ca site was launched a few years later. The site is easy to navigate allowing you to search on contests based on time-frames such

as Daily, Weekly, One Time Only, etc. What makes this site interesting is many of the contests listed are not limited to Canadians. A lot of the contests listed are open to both Americans and Canadians along with listings for global or worldwide promotions. So, you may find some contests here that are not listed on other sites. There is a free membership available, allowing you to login and keep track of your contests in My Contests.

You can also sign-up for his free e-newsletter which comes out approximately twice a week. (www.contesthound.ca/newsletter.php 3?siteID=edge) The newsletter always features a story about his kids and his life as a stay-at-home, work-at-home dad. Very funny!

Free Contests ⊠

www.freecontests.ca
This is Canada's newest contesting site. It is one of the many websites created and managed by CanadianSponsors.com (www.canadiansponsors.com). Creative Director James Walker created Free Contests as a means to increase awareness of his client's promotional campaigns. You can sign-up for a free weekly e-newsletter featuring new contests listed on their site. New promotions can be submitted via their sister site, www.canadafreestuff.ca.

Frugal Shopper⊠

www.frugalshopper.ca
Kimberly Clancy started Frugal Shopper as a hobby in 2001. Its initial focus was where to find sales and freebies. The contest section grew out of the freebie section, www.frugalshopper.ca/contests/index.asp. You can sign-up for a free monthly newsletter featuring contests, freebies, and coupons both on and off line.

Quebec Concours

www.quebecconcours.com
NOTE: This site is in French.
Marc Gagnon started searching the Internet one night for contests open to Quebec residents because his girlfriend was frustrated at the lack of resources for Quebecois contesters. Along with Yassine Bichri (co-owner of www.sekooya.com) they launched Quebec Concours. The

website has an extensive list of online contests, sweepstakes, lotteries and even surveys that pay participants. Although the site audience is mainly from Quebec, all Canadian provinces are welcome to participate in all of the listed contests since they are valid nationwide. Participants can win cash, vacations, cars, electronics, movies, gift certificates and more. You can access their English website here: www.canadasweepstakes.ca.

Somewhere In Canada ✉
www.somewhereincanada.com/contests/
Shannon Shoemaker started Somewhere in Canada in 2000. It not only lists contests but there are a lot of good resources such as Tips, FAQs, and a Glossary of contesting terms. The site has contests broken down by type and region, and allows a contestor to save links and check back on a regular basis for new promotions. Sign-up for the Contest Club to share contest information with others in an email format.

Shannon and her husband, Vince Pelss, own an information technology company called Emogic www.emogic.com. They wrote the software packages Rewards™ and Barcode UPC Personal Assistant™ (BUPA), which are reviewed in this book.

Wanna Win ✉
www.wannawin.ca
Wanna Win is owned and managed by Mastodonte Communications Inc. in Montreal. If you sign-up for their free membership you will receive their e-newsletter. It is sent out approximately every two weeks and only if there is a new promotion.

www.toutacoup.ca is the French counterpart to Wanna Win. They also operate: www.toutacoup.fr, www.toutacoup.be and www.wannawin.us.

Text Messaging
TXT (Text Messaging) or SMS (Short Message Service) on your cell phone is the newest form of contesting. If you have not begun entering via your cell phone, you should start. Relatively few people enter these contests (compared to other methods of entering sweepstakes), so your

odds of winning are very good. My husband or I have won a prize from almost every SMS contest we have entered so far.

There are two types of SMS contests: ones that are only entered via your cell phone, and ones that have an SMS entry component to them.

Always read the rules of every contest to see what the different entry methods are. If SMS messaging is an option, use it—if the only method of entry is via your cell phone, the odds of winning are the best of all the contest entry methods at this time, and if it is a component of a contest, it will usually garner you extra entries into the contest.

Many people do not have a messaging package with their wireless provider and are afraid to enter because each message could cost 25¢ or more. Yet, those same people will mail off dozens of entries into a promotion at 50¢ per letter. Call your cell phone service provider and sign-up for a SMS messaging package today. (I currently pay $10.00 per month for 200 messages—a bargain when you consider what some contestors spend on postage.)

Since each cell phone is different, I suggest you read the manual for specific instructions on how to use your phone's messaging service. Here is a link for SMS short forms to help you get started. www.techdictionary.com/chatsms.html

My husband, Craig, won our first prize from an SMS messaging contest. He won an "In The Action" game package consisting of two In The Action Seats to a specified Toronto Jays game, the opportunity to watch the team warm up, a "Behind The Scenes" tour of Rogers Centre, an official Jays jersey which he got autographed by three players, a golf shirt, two baseball hats and a Super Sports Pack twelve month subscription from Rogers Cable.

My father-in-law, Len, is a HUGE baseball fan and flew in from British Columbia to join Craig at the practice and game. This so impressed the Jays' marketing staff that they also gave Len an official Jays jersey (increasing the value of the win).

TIP: It never hurts to ask. It was at my request they threw in the extra Jersey. It is up to the discretion of the contest sponsor to change or alter the prize.

Profession or Hobby?

pro·fes·sion·al (prə-fĕsh**ʹ**ə-nəl)

adj.　　**1. a.** Of, relating to, engaged in, or suitable for a profession: *lawyers, doctors, and other professional people.*

b. Conforming to the standards of a profession: *professional behavior.*

2. Engaging in a given activity as a source of livelihood or as a career: *a professional writer.*

3. Performed by persons receiving pay: *professional football.*

4. Having or showing great skill; expert: *a professional repair job.*

n.　　**1.** A person following a profession, especially a learned profession.

2. One who earns a living in a given or implied occupation: *hired a professional to decorate the house.*

3. A skilled practitioner; an expert.

hob·by (hŏb**ʹ**ē)

n. pl. **hob·bies** An activity or interest pursued outside one's regular occupation and engaged in primarily for pleasure.

63

What is an enthusiastic contestor called? I have been called a professional contestor. The term makes me uncomfortable because a professional is an expert in a specific field and is usually well paid for their skill and knowledge. I consider contesting to be a hobby because 1) it is not my main occupation, 2) I do it for pleasure, and 3) I certainly could not live off my winnings.

There are several terms used globally to describe someone who enters contests on a regular basis. In Canada we refer to ourselves as contestors because we enter contests. In the United States they refer to themselves as sweepers because they enter sweepstakes. (If we did that in Canada, they would think we were curlers!) In the United Kingdom and Australia they refer to themselves as competitors because they enter competitions. As Shakespeare said, "A rose by any other name would smell as sweet." My favorite term to describe my hobby is *winner*.

Do you consider contesting to be your hobby?

Many of us do. What makes the following article the most interesting to me is the statistic at the end by Decima Research.

> If you have three minutes to spare, you could win a new car, and all it takes is the push of a button. Sound too good to be true? It isn't. From now until January 3, 2005, GM Canada is giving away 150 cars to 150 lucky Canadians who simply visit their local GM dealership and push the GM Hot Button. The GM Hot Button promotion is open to all Canadians who have reached the age of majority and have a driver's license. Here's how it works:
> - Visit any participating GM dealer and push the blue OnStar button in a designated GM Hot Button vehicle.

- After providing some basic information a random prize response announces exactly what you've won.
- If you don't win one of the 150 vehicles, you could win $2,000 to $10,000 off the purchase or lease of a new vehicle, and at a minimum, all eligible participants will be awarded either $1,000 or $500 off the purchase or lease of most 2005 and 2004 models.

GM Hot Button makes it easy to win, but according to a poll conducted by Decima Research, Canadians would do just about anything for a chance at a new set of wheels:

- 61 per cent of Canadians say they would give up sex for a week for a chance to win a car;
- 80 per cent of Canadians would give up fast food;
- 76 per cent would give up television;
- 70 per cent would give up Internet usage.
- 17 per cent of Canadians would eat a plate of worms for a chance to win a new vehicle;
- Over one third (37 per cent) would sing to a stadium full of people;
- 13 per cent would run around the block naked and 31 per cent would move back home with their parents.
- Almost half (47 per cent) of Canadians say they would wait in a lineup for an hour for a chance to win a new vehicle;
- 13 per cent would wait a full day or longer.

To find your local GM dealer, visit <www.gmcanada.com> or call 1-800-GM-DRIVE. Do You Feel Lucky?

Did you know just one third (33 per cent) of Canadians say they enter draws, sweepstakes or contests. But of those who do, almost one third (32 per cent) report that they have won something.

Reprinted with permission from *The Community Press*, December 8th 2004 - www.communitypress-online.com

*"Luck is what happens when
preparation meets opportunity."
Darrell Royal*

MY INTERNET
CONTESTING SYSTEM

The following Internet contest entering system was created, adjusted, and expanded to its current format over a four year period.

NOTE: The secret to any system is CONSISTENCY. I enter contests EVERY DAY, 7 days per week. Remember: to win prizes on a consistent basis, you need to enter on a consistent basis. (There are some odd days I don't enter any contests due to a busy life but they are few and far between.)

NOTE: On average it takes about 90 days before you begin to win because the contests you enter today will not be drawn for a few weeks. Don't let this short lag discourage you—keep entering, and the wins will come.

Entering Online

This section assumes a working knowledge of computers and basic software packages. If you are new to computers or would like to learn more about computer basics, I recommend reading Windows for Dummies. (*Be sure to read the book relating to the version of Microsoft Windows® on your PC.*) I will give you a brief overview of the system followed by detailed examples.

NOTE FOR MAC USERS: The Internet Contesting System is the same except that the specialty contesting software described below is currently not available for Macs. The system I describe using a web browser to find and track contests will work for you, but you will likely have to enter forms manually instead of having an application to fill them out for you.

I divide all the contests I come across into four groups: daily, weekly, monthly and one-time-only entry. These categories make it easier to enter and help avoid accidental disqualification. I originally used Microsoft Internet Explorer® (IE) as my Internet browser and contest tracker. When I purchased a faster PC, I added RoboForm as my auto-form filler. I will be discussing alternative programs and software packages later in the book. (see *Alternative Online Entry Systems.*)

IE has a feature called FAVORITES, which allows you to save and organize webpage addresses (also called URLs, which stands for Uniform Resource Locator). This was the basis for my system. When I would find a new contest online, I began by saving the link in Favorites into a folder called Contests. As the list grew, I began to get confused as to when a contest ended and how many people in the house could enter. I found myself making mistakes, such as entering contests that had already closed. That is how my four folder system began.

NOTE: You can use this contest organization system in the Netscape, Firefox, Opera, or Safari browsers using Bookmarks and Folders. Other browsers use the term 'bookmark' where Internet Explorer calls them 'favorites,' but regardless of the naming they all allow you to save URLs so that you can go back to the website later.

I created four folders with obvious names:
- Daily
- Weekly
- Monthly
- One Time Only

As I found out about new contests I would go to the entry page and read the rules to determine end date, number of entries per household and the entry period. I would then save the URL to the appropriate folder with a new name, the contest end date and the number of people I could enter.

Once I added RoboForm it dramatically sped up the time it took me to fill out an online entry form—I could now enter as many as 200+ ballots in a given day. WOW!

NOTE: You only need to set up the One Time Entry folder if you elect to enter those contests later in the entry period. If you will be entering one time only contests as soon as you find them, then this folder is not required.

TIP: Enter Daily contests every day, Weekly contests on a specific day of the week such as every Monday, and Monthly and One Time Only contests on the first and/or the fifteenth of the month. That way you will always remember when to enter.

Let me review the system in more detail. Have your four folders set-up in your Favorites before you begin saving contest links and bring them to the top of your list. I will use a non-contest site for this example as real contest sites can change on a daily basis.

For example, you are watching TV, reading a magazine or receive a contest link via email and decide to visit the site to check out the contest. You go to www.contestqueen.com and see a contest for a trip around the world.

The **first thing** you do is **read the rules**. There are several things you are scanning for:

- the contest entry period (e.g. June 1, 2005 to December 31, 2005)
- the region the contest is open to (e.g. open to all residents of Canada)
- age restrictions (e.g. persons who are the age of majority or more within the province in which they reside)
- how many people per household can enter (e.g. one entry per person or email address),

- how often you can enter (e.g. once per day, once per week, etc…)

If you do not meet all of the contest requirements, even if your name is drawn you will not win. I cannot stress the importance of this enough—I have disqualified myself many times in the past because I rushed reading the rules.

Once you have determined the contest criteria you save the link in the appropriate folder. For our example, suppose the contest is running from August 1, 2005 until September 30, 2005, is open to all residents of Canada who are the age of majority or more in the

province in which they reside, and allows one entry per household per 24 hour period. CLICK on FAVORITES, then on ADD TO FAVORITES. A window will pop-up with a Name and Folder list.

TIP: You can either leave the name as it appears in the field; "Contest Queen" or you can change it to something you would remember such as "Around the World Trip".

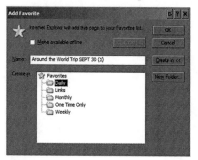

Type the end date of the contest after the name followed by the number of contestants. **Around the World Trip SEPT 30 (1)** SELECT the Daily folder in the Create in window and click on OK. Now, when you are in IE and you select FAVORITES, DAILY you will notice your new shortcut to the contest entry page has been added to the bottom of the list. Select it and move it into end-date order, with the contests ending soonest at the top.

TIP: Having your contests in end-date order will allow you to enter those that are ending shortly first. This is important for the days you may not have as much time to contest so you can get the most entries in as possible per contest.

As the contest end dates arrive, enter the contest and delete the link on the last day. If you are contesting on a consistent basis you will always have an evolving list of contests to enter. Since companies are moving away from mail-in contests to online contesting, I always have a list that has no less than 50 contests at any given time—I have had it as large as 125. To delete a contest, use the right mouse button and click on the contest link you wish to remove. A pop-up menu will appear. Select DELETE and click the left mouse button and SELECT Yes. If you accidentally delete a link, you can always retrieve it from your Recycle Bin if you haven't emptied it.

TIP: To avoid confusion when entering more than one person into a contest, always enter everyone in the same order. (e.g. yourself, spouse, sister, brother, daughter, son, etc...)

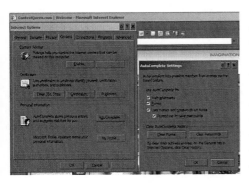

TIP: Ensure AutoComplete is activated in IE. In IE, CLICK on TOOLS, INTERNET OPTIONS, CONTENT and in the Personal Information section, CLICK on AUTOCOMPLETE. Ensure Web Addresses, Forms and User Names and Passwords on Form

71

*are checked. Then CLICK OK and select MY PROFILE. Go through every TAB and fill in all your personal information. **IE for Macs has a similar auto-fill feature.** This feature will enable IE to fill in this data for you automatically so you don't have to type it each time—a real time saver.*

Mail-in vs Online

I have been asked by many people what types of prizes have I won from online contests. To date, 85% of my wins are from online promotions. I have won everything from CDs, DVDs, movie passes, t-shirts and baseball hats, to a year supply of bubble gum, a set of cookware, running shoes and several vacations. The list seems endless.

Early in my hobby I entered an online contest sponsored by a poultry company. They had an early bird draw (pardon the pun) and my husband won. It was a weekend at the Molson Indy car race in gold grandstand seats, all the chicken he could eat, free t-shirts and hats, plus a hot lap around the track in a pace car. Craig got to go down Lakeshore Blvd. (in Toronto) at 190 MPH! This was a great win for him because he is a huge race fan.

I have also had the pleasure of meeting Michael Bublé and Sting.

TIP: Set up an email account that you only use on contest entry forms/ballots. You can either set one up with your Internet service provider or you can use a free web-based service (e.g. Hotmail, Yahoo or Gmail).

TIP: Use the same username and 6+ character password for all your online contest entries. For security reasons, do not use the same ones for personal or business use—that way, if someone gets your contesting username and password, they can't use it to access your bank accounts.

Ongoing Contests

There are websites that always have lists of ongoing contests. (see *Internet.*) They are usually split into two categories: Daily or Weekly.

www.tribute.ca is a good example of a website that has continuously ongoing daily entry contests. They are in my folder as: Tribute DAILY.

The websites you will want to check on a weekly basis are your local television, radio stations and newspapers. The specific websites will vary from region to region. Even though most of us can now watch television stations from across the country via satellite/cable or listen to any radio station around the world via the Internet, most small prizes are for local events, or must be picked up in person. As a result, it only makes sense to enter locally. In my Weekly folder I have the links to all the major television stations, radio stations and newspapers in my area. Most contests are one entry only per person so having them in my Weekly folder allows me to check these sites frequently.

One Time Only

I like these contests the best because I feel the playing field is level since everyone has an equal chance. I may be biased since many of the contests I have won have been from single entry contests. There are two theories to entering these contests: some people enter as soon as they hear about a contest, and others wait until the contest has been running for some time. I have tried both over the past several years and I can't definitively say that I have won more one way or the other. You can decide for yourself which way you prefer to enter.

If you choose to enter sometime during the contest period, your link saving method is almost the same. The only difference is, after you read the rules and discover what the entry period is, select as many dates as you wish to enter for yourself, your spouse, and other family members or friends using their initials as a marker. So using our example from before, the entry would read **Around the World AUG 15 CRW SEPT 1 CWB SEP 15 NPW**.

This would enter myself (CRW), my husband (CWB), and my daughter (NPW) at various intervals throughout the contest. After the contest entry date passes for the first person and they have been entered, use the right mouse button to select the contest. This will bring up the pop-up menu and select RENAME. Erase the first entry date and initials and click on OK. This will leave it in the One Time Only folder for the next date, when you will enter the next person in the contest (see *High-Speed Online Entries* about adding and using multiple Identities in RoboForm to speed-up entry process.) It is important to remember to remove the names as you enter various people, so that you do not enter anyone more than once and disqualify them.

NOTE: If you enter family and friends into contests on their behalf, ensure that you have an agreement with them in advance if they win, that they will share the prize with you (e.g. trip for four). I have heard many stories of family members no longer speaking or friendships souring because of something that was suppose to be fun going awry.

STORY: Susan submitted a good example of forewarning your friends about entering their names into contests. I am glad they are still friends.

৪৩

Susan—Calgary, AB

I entered a contest a while ago and one of the requirements was that I tell a story about someone who inspired me. I had no clue, so I put down a friend's name in, and told a quickie little blurb about her. I still have no idea what I wrote; I just wanted to enter the contest so I could potentially win something. Well, low and behold, I won—received the following in an email:

> "At (our company), we recognize there are many inspirational stories of remarkable women across Canada who are making great contributions to society and going above and beyond to encourage, mentor and provide leadership. That's why we've created a program to recognize these women that have been active in their community and have shown exemplary leadership in all facets of their lives.
>
> "A national call for submissions was recently held requesting nominations of remarkable women across Canada. Your remarkable woman submission was chosen to be one of the hundred we will honour with a very special gift."

Well, let me tell you, my friend was none too pleased that I didn't know what I had wrote, but she ended up getting quite a nice little present out of it—a really nice daytimer worth close to $100.

My friend certainly thought it was funny—she didn't care about the daytimer, she wanted to know what I had written about her—but I can't for the life of me remember. I was in contesting mode, entering everything I could find. On top of that, I didn't think to ask the person who called a few days later to confirm the information I had sent. So, my friend is pleased with me, but annoyed at the same time. Lesson learned.

৪৩

Opt-In or Opt-Out?

Many online contest entry forms have what is known as OPT-IN or OPT-OUT statements.

EXAMPLE:

☐ **Yes**, I would like to receive occasional, promotional announcements from ACME Inc.

☐ **Yes**, I would like to receive occasional promotional announcements from Contest Management Inc., the contest hosting company.

If you click on the box, you are opting-in. If you leave it blank, you are opting-out.

Companies use these check boxes to create prospect databases—when you opt-in, you are giving your permission for them to send you information at a later date on their products or services. To potentially reduce Spam, always opt-out. However, as the example shows, many companies offer either advance or start-date notification of new contests and promotions. If you wish to receive those notifications, opt-in. You can always cancel your subscription if you do not like it.

TIP: Read the rules, because some promotions require you to opt-in in order to receive an entry into the contest or you may receive bonus entries.

Filling Out Online Forms Faster

As I stated earlier, RoboForm cut my contesting time in half, because I no longer had to fill out every online contest entry form manually, (i.e. type out my personal contact information over and over and over...)

When you first install RoboForm, you will be asked to fill out an Identity. When you go to a page with a form, RoboForm launches a small pop-up window with a list of all the Identities you have added to the program. It is simply a matter of selecting the Identity and clicking on either FILL or FILL & SUBMIT. You will then see all the personal data for that person auto-fill on the form.

It is important to note the difference between Fill and Fill & Submit. You will use Fill & Submit when the page is a plain ordinary entry form page. (see *High-speed Online Entries* to see how you can speed the Fill & Submit process up even faster!) You will use Fill when the page is not in Flash and has a two-step entry process, an authentication code or multiple frames, because if you use Fill & Submit you will get an entry error.

NOTE: Flash is a development environment made by Macromedia (www.macromedia.com) for creating web content. It allows developers to add animation and interactive content to a webpage. This matters to us as contestors because RoboForm and other automated form filler applications will not recognize forms that are written in Flash. If the contest uses a Flash based form, you will have to enter the data manually. Entering online contest entry forms based in Flash will increase your time spent entering online contests because you must manually enter all your personal information.

High-Speed Online Entries

I added to my Internet Contesting System when I had begun researching my book and came across more and more contest related software packages.

RoboForm Companion was a fantastic discovery. It auto-enters any Passcard you have created in RoboForm for plain entry forms (not those in Flash, having authentication or verification codes, have a two-step entry process or have multiple frames) and can cut your online contest entry time dramatically. (*See below for details on what to do with Flash sites.*)

The Passcard feature in RoboForm is the secret to using RoboForm Companion. When RoboForm Companion opens it also opens all the Passcards that have been saved in RoboForm. That's why it is important to: 1) purchase RoboForm Pro so you have unlimited Passcards and, 2) learn to use the Passcard feature immediately after learning the basic auto form fill function on RoboForm because it will greatly speed up your online contest entering process.

It was very easy to integrate RoboForm Companion into my daily routine because I only had to make a few minor system modifications. I began by separating all the contests with entry pages that had straight forward online forms vs. those that had two step entries, required verification codes, or were in Flash.

I began by saving Passcards for standard form pages with either a **D** for daily or a **W** for weekly entries. (There is no need to use RoboForm Companion with one time entry contests.) Once RoboForm Companion is opened, all the Passcards are listed in alphabetical order on the left hand side of the screen, so it is important to place a D or a W at the beginning so that all the Daily and Weekly entries will be grouped together. Everyday when I enter my Daily contests, I highlight all the Ds and click on SUBMIT. On Mondays, I do all the Ws in the same manner. RoboForm Companion will then go from Passcard to Passcard entering the contest for you automatically. While it is running in the background, I use IE to enter all the contests I must enter manually.

TIP: You can also use the Passcard feature for other types of online entries, such as when a form has more than the standard name, address, and phone number fields to be filled out on a regular basis. For example, a survey or two-step entry process will require you to enter additional information, yet the first part can still be filled by RoboForm.

NOTE: Passcards can also be used with Turbo Sweeps or Sweeps.

You start by manually filling out the online form ensuring that all the fields are filled out accurately and then within RoboForm, CLICK on PASSCARD. A Save Passcard—RoboForm window will appear for you to name and save the Passcard.

If the Passcard is to be used with RoboForm Companion, save the Passcard as **D Around the World Trip CRW** (or with a W at the beginning depending on the entry requirements). Save subsequent Passcards for all the people you would like to enter on either a daily or a weekly basis. If the form is to be manually submitted, just save it as **Around the World Trip CRW**.

I continue to use my system of saving the contest in Favorites so I know when a contest expires. If it is to be entered by RoboForm Companion the system remains the same. If I am to

ENTER Wide Screen TV Contest NOV 11 (2)
ENTER Zathura -NOV 13 (3)
ENTER HomeSense NOV 13 (1)
ENTER Six Degrees of Separation NOV 15 (2)
ENTER Home Depot NOV 15 (2)
ENTER Britney Spears Fantasy NOV 15 (1)

manually enter the contest, I add the word ENTER in front of the name so it now looks like this example: **ENTER Trip to NYC DEC 31 (2)**.

The RoboForm Companion software package is a lifesaver on days I would otherwise have no time to enter any contests. In the past, I would have entered none, but now I am at least entering what I can with RoboForm Companion. (I average 100+ ballots in RoboForm Companion on a daily basis.)

NOTE: If a contest page opens and the RoboForm window does not appear, the form is probably in Flash. You will need to type all the data in manually for this type of form each and every time for each and every person. More and more companies are using Flash based forms because: 1) the website can be more interactive, "hipper", etc. and 2) it slows the avid contestor down.

Alternative Online Entry Systems

Turbo Sweeps and Sweep are packages I will mention here even though I do not use them as part of my Internet Contesting System. I cover both as part of my course, How To Win Cash Cars Trips & More, because I think many people may benefit from the great features these software packages have.

I believe that had I discovered Turbo Sweeps or Sweep earlier, I may have developed my system around one of those software packages, but by the time I discovered them I had gotten so comfortable with my routine and the packages I was using I felt no need to change.

TIP: Turbo Sweeps and Sweep will electronically track all your contests in a similar format to Part One of my Internet Contesting System. (see Contesting Software.)

STORY: Through writing this book I met many women like Wanda. I am using the title Contest Queen for marketing myself and this book. Wanda really is a Contest Queen!

இଓଔ

Wanda—Winnipeg, MB
I am 50 years old, the happily married mom of two teenage boys. The first contest I entered was when I was 16 years old. I remember I won an LP record by a popular musical group. I didn't really do too much with contests again until about two years later and then entered the odd one here and there and won a few neat things. Over the years I became more adept at finding contests learning where to look for them, trading forms with friends and subscribing to contesting newsletters.

I used to speak to ladies' groups on How to Win Contests and it always went over well. However, that was almost ten years ago and everything I taught referred to mail-ins, in-stores, radio contests—*not* Internet contests. Times have changed!

I now prefer to enter online contests but continue to enter in-store draws and mail-ins, as well. With in-store draws, I try to throw a few entries in each store of whichever chain is giving away a particular prize. I fold my forms in various unique ways and I enter as often as possible. With mail-ins, I make sure to enter every contest at least once and for larger prizes, increasing to as many entries as I can afford postage for.

I subscribe to a couple of online contesting newsletters and pay for a mail-in contesting newsletter which arrives in my email box on a regular basis. I also find contests on my own by surfing the web. I like to use Google to search Canadian web pages and I type in phrases (in quotation marks) such as "enter as often as you wish," "one entry per person," "win a," "rules and regulations," "deadline for entries," and "open to residents of Canada."

I love sharing information in my online groups because I believe what goes around comes around. Occasionally, I will enter contests based out of the U.S. which are also open to Canadian residents, but usually only when the prize is something I really want. This is because prizes coming across the border into Canada require a GST fee to be paid. With Canadian contests, I try to enter everything that I can. When Internet contests first became available it was a little discouraging when I would read "only one entry per day," whereas I could previously mail in more than that. When I think back, I don't really recall mailing anything in that often except for only the odd contest and then only for prizes I really wouldn't have minded having (and it wasn't always a guarantee that I'd win). With most Internet contests, you are allowed to enter once per day and by doing so you can get in a lot more entries than by only mailing in a few now and then. Even when a contest says one entry per person, I will still enter because at least then everyone has the same chance. It could just as easily be me who wins as anybody else.

NOTE: Wanda's full description of her contesting system is very similar to mine so I won't repeat it here.

TIP FROM WANDA: If there is a UPC code or answer to a skill-testing question that needs to be inserted into an entry each day, I'll add that info in brackets somewhere in the file name I create in IE Favorites. I don't list all the prizes in my file names, only the top prize in each contest. That way if I only have a few minutes one day to enter contests I can scan through my bookmarks and only enter the best ones.

I type like the wind so I can get entry forms filled in quite quickly. I often use the auto-fill feature of my Google Toolbar to fill in my forms so it speeds up the process even further. I spend approximately 1½ hours contesting on a daily basis.

YOU CAN'T WIN IF YOU DON'T ENTER

NOTE: See Contesting Software for other programs that can assist you in entering online forms more quickly.

I miss the mail-in contests because I could sit down whenever I had spare time and prepare all the entries I planned to mail in for each contest, all at once, and then just throw a few in the mailbox every day. On the other hand, Internet contests are great because you can enter almost every day, get in a lot of entries and not have to pay the postage.

NOTE: Wanda also included a partial list of her wins over the years. I will only highlight a few of the prizes since her list was so long. Good for you, Wanda!!

- trip for two to the Bahamas
- European tour for two
- trip for 2 to the Olympics in Barcelona, Spain
- trip for 4 to Universal Studios/Disneyland
- trip for 2 to Puerto Vallarta, Mexico
- golfing trip for 2 to Whistler, B.C.
- golfing trip for 2 to Kelowna, B.C.
- trip for 2 to Rome, Italy
- 1923 Model T Ford
- 10-speed bicycle
- 12-speed bicycle
- toys of all types
- $3500 cash
- books of all types
- tickets to all sorts of events
- many gift certificates
- set of Royal Doulton china
- lots and lots of movie passes
- microwave oven
- too many t-shirts to count
- cell phone
- camping equipment
- set of golf clubs
- gas barbecue
- year's supply of pantyhose

Wanda says, "There are countless other things, but it's impossible for me to remember everything because I've been doing this for so many years."

౸෪

"The only sure thing about luck is that it will change."
Bret Harte

CONTESTING SOFTWARE

When I began entering contests online I would enter every form manually. It was *very* time consuming. I noticed people in the groups chatting about RoboForm, an auto-form filling software package, but I hesitated to use it because I was afraid if I used form-filling software my entry would be disqualified. (Sometimes contest rules state that if you are found to have used an automated contest entry service, similar to acuwin.com, you would be disqualified.) I also had a fairly slow computer without much memory, and another program just might have crashed my system.

In December of 2002 it became apparent my computer had even become too slow to run our business. So, I broke down and got a new computer and boy, was it fast!! I could get through my contests in much less time. I started thinking about the auto-form filling software again. I emailed a few people in the I Can Win group and was assured using a form-filler in no way would disqualify me, so I downloaded RoboForm. *It cut my contesting time in half!!* I was hooked.

NOTE: As with any new software package, integrating it into your daily routine does take time to set-up and to adapt to the intricacies of the package. Be patient during this process—it will pay off many times over.

In April of 2005 I found another fantastic timesaving software package; RoboForm Companion. It was recommended to me by Tom Stamatson of About.com. He found it very useful so I thought I would give it a try. *WOW!!* It uses the Passcards in RoboForm to auto-enter form based contest entries. Again, my contesting time was cut in half. (I am now down to only an hour or two of online contesting per day, as opposed to three or four, with the time I save using RoboForm and RoboForm Companion.)

85

Other contestors *love* using Turbo Sweep or Sweep because of their ability to track contest entries. This can be especially helpful if the promotion is one entry per person or household for the entire entry period, because most contests will disqualify you for duplicate entries and many promotions do not use Repeat Entry Blocks. (see *Contest Development & Management Companies*.) As I have mentioned before, I have based my system around RoboForm and RoboForm Companion, but don't take this as saying that these are *better* than Sweep or Turbo Sweep—try them for yourself, and determine which approach you like best.

To maximize the number of entries you can submit on any given day, I recommend you use one or more time saving software packages. It was through talking to others and taking advantage of free trial offers that I came to know about and love the various contesting tools I currently use. Remember, all software packages can be removed from your computer if you do not find them useful.

NOTE: Most of these packages offer a free trial period. If you like a package, buy it. Buying a software package you like and use everyday is worth every penny. I believe it is good karma to support the software developers if the package helps you. (see Attracting Luck.) It will also encourage them to design and create newer and more innovative software to keep up with ever evolving contest entry forms. Support those who make good tools, and they will support you back.

Is This Legal??

The contest rules sometimes state an automated entry is illegal. My original fear was using auto-form filling software would be considered an automated entry and I would be disqualified. This is not the case because you are entering the contest from *your* computer. The system cannot tell if you manually typed in your personal information or a form filler did it for you. All it does is save your fingers from retyping the same data over and over again.

An automated entry is submitted when you pay a company, such as Acuwin, to enter promotions for you. Contest sponsors do not like automated entries because it defeats the purpose of their promotion; to get you excited about their product or service by participating in their contest yourself. Even using RoboForm Companion does not disqualify you because you are entering every promotion, form by form, from *your* computer. You still need to go to the contest entry site to set up the Passcard (and to read the contest rules, of course...), so the company is still getting your attention. Automated entry systems like Acuwin are completely different, in that you may never see the promotion or even know which contests you are entering with those services.

NOTE: Any prices quoted below were correct at the time of printing and are subject to change.

BUPA (Barcode UPC Personal Assistant)

www.emogic.com/software/freeware/bupa/index.html
BUPA allows you to organize, share, display and print UPC codes. It is a very useful program for those who enter contests requiring a UPC. This program replaces the many files of product packages and UPCs contestors used to keep. Just enter the UPCs into the software and it is stored for future use. The number is then easily retrieved to be entered into an online contest form requiring a UPC. If you are entering a mail-in contest that requires a UPC, you can print out the barcode and either freehand a reasonable facsimile or trace it. This program is free of charge. A donation of $15.00 is appreciated.

Code	Company	Product	Size	Description	Bought in	Date Entered
0-63000452685	Schneiders	Hot Stuffs	256g	Smoked Ham and Cheddar	Yes	8/31/2001
0-620008021 7-6	Schneiders	Chicken Pies	Unknown		Yes	1/29/2001
0-6210000981-9	Cadbury Beverages Canada	Canada Dry	case 24 X355		Yes	1/21/2001
0-62187000403-9	Advil	Ibuprofen	8 tablets		Yes	9/29/2001
0-62187187947	Whitehall Robins	Centrum Forte	100 tablets	Multivitamin-Multimineral Formula	Yes	1/4/2001

Rewards

www.emogic.com/software/freeware/rewards/index.html
Rewards allows you to enter in a contest URL, how often you would like to enter it and when the contest is over. To start, select SHOW TO DO. You get a list of what contests you would like to enter. It is then a matter of going down the list, clicking on GO TO SITE, filling out the entry form, clicking MARK AS DONE then NEXT TO DO. It is very easy to use. To auto-fill forms, you can use Rewards in conjunction

with RoboForm. This software is free of charge. A donation of $15.00 is appreciated.

NOTE: Once you launch Rewards, click on REGISTER. You will then get an INVALID CODE message. Click PROCEED to enter the program.

RoboForm

www.RoboForm.com/?addid=im123

NOTE: Type in the code QUEEN to receive a 10% discount when purchasing RoboForm.

This software is a must for every contestor! RoboForm is a Password Manager and a Web Form Filler software package. It completely automates the password entering and form filling process. It does this by allowing you to add in Identities with all of the data usually found on online entry forms. (Name, Address, Telephone Number, Birth Date, etc…) When you open a webpage that has a form RoboForm can fill, a pop-up window appears with all your Identities. You can then select a name (Identity) and fill the form with one click.

If a form has many more fields, such as a short survey, fill in the entire page, save it as a Passcard and every time you return to that particular webpage, you can fill the whole entry with just one click. Passcards also memorize the URL of the form that you have filled. This allows you to use the GO FILL toolbar command or the GO TO in the Passcard Editor to navigate your browser to a particular web page with the contest entry form, and automatically fill the form from the Passcard.

RoboForm also has a portable version called Pass2Go that resides on a USB memory stick. It allows you to take your Identities and Passcards with you everywhere. This is especially helpful for the contestor that does not have their own computer and must rely on family, friends or the public library for computer/Internet access.

RoboForm works on most pages except those built with Flash. It can be used to speed-up the data entry of forms that have verification codes, are part of a two-step entry process or have multiple frames on the page. (see *Filling Out Online Forms Faster*.)

RoboForm Pro is $29.95 USD and $14.95 USD for Pass2Go. There is a 30-day money back guarantee and all future upgrades are free of charge.

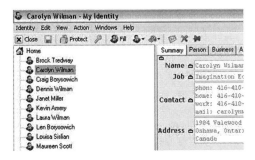

NOTE: The free version of RoboForm will only allow you to have ten Passcards. If you choose to use RoboForm Companion in conjunction with RoboForm, you will need to buy RoboForm Pro. (I have an average of 100+ Passcards I use within RoboForm Companion at any given time.)

TIP: Always use the Fill and then manually submit option the first time entering a contest after creating a Passcard. Some contests have a pop-up agree-to-the-rules feature and you may not be entering properly with the fill and submit feature.

RoboForm Companion

www.cydrix.com

RoboForm Companion was created in 2002 by Vincent Lavoie, CEO of Cydrix Solutions. His brother and father are contestors and needed an easier way to submit their forms. With his programming experience, knowledge of the Internet, and understanding of a contestor's mentality, he was able to create a program that works hand-in-hand with RoboForm.

As with any new software package, it took me a few days of playing around with it to understand how it would work best for me. It has cut my daily contest entry time in half! The only reason it is not able to do all my daily contest entries is it only works with form based entries. (see *High-speed Online Entries*, for further information on how it fits into my daily routine.) If a contest uses certain types of password fields, agreement pop-ups or is designed in Flash, it will not work. I continue to go to those types of entry forms daily and fill them out manually.

RoboForm Companion has a 30-day trial period, which is wonderful, because it will allow you to try it and determine if it right for you. It is $15.00 USD for a one year subscription. I feel it is a very good value.

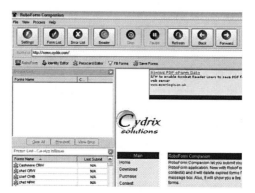

NOTE: Sweep and Turbo Sweeps are very similar software packages. The main difference is that Sweep runs over a standard web browser

like Internet Explorer, whereas Turbo Sweeps has its own integrated web browser.

Sweep

www.wavget.com/sweep.html

Sweep allows you to keep detailed records of all the online sweepstakes, contests and promotions you enter electronically. Once launched, it opens a small window over Internet Explorer. You record the start and end dates of the promotion and how often you can enter along with any notes/comments such as UPCs. Sweep will also track your number of entries into a given contest. This package is very good for someone wishing to keep all of their online contesting information in one place. Sweep is free of charge.

NOTE: RoboForm also works in conjunction with Sweep.

Turbo Sweeps

www.turbosweeps.com

Turbo Sweeps allows you to keep detailed records of all the online sweepstakes, contest and promotions you enter electronically. What makes it unique is it's an integrated web browser *and* sweepstakes manager along with organizing and scheduling your required entries. You enter the contest URL in the Turbo Sweeps browser and save all the required contest data into the information dialog box. Then each time you return, Turbo Sweeps allows you to see what you need to enter that day. Contests can be saved in a similar manner to my system:

Daily, Weekly, Monthly, One Time Only, etc., which makes it perfect for someone that needs to be organized and only wishes to use one software package. Turbo Sweeps is free of charge.

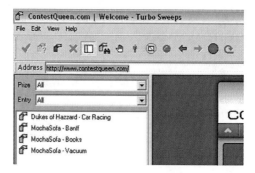

NOTE: RoboForm also works within Turbo Sweeps if you do not wish to use their Smart Fill or Turbo Fill features

Acuwin
http://acuwin.com
Acuwin is the largest automated entry service on the Internet. You pay them a monthly fee ($4.95 - $9.95 USD per month) and they guarantee your entry in thousands of sweepstakes.

I do not recommend you use Acuwin (or any other similar service) because using their services constitutes an automated entry and may disqualify you from most of the promotions you have paid them to enter on your behalf. This is also a US–based company and will not have many contests open to Canadians.

NOTE: Using my Internet Contesting System (or a similar one) will allow you to 1) enjoy the hobby of contesting and 2) enter you into far more promotions than a service can provide. I average 6000+ entries per month as opposed to the 2000+ offered by Acuwin.

Posting to groups
www.makeashorterlink.com
www.tinyurl.com

These sites offer a very handy tool for contestors. You can take a very long URL and shorten it down. You would want to use these sites when posting messages to online groups because sometimes a URL may become unclickable when it "wraps" within the message. This saves others viewing the message from having to cut and paste the URL in their browser or figuring out another way to get to the entry page. It will also save you time when others do the same for you.

EXAMPLES:

Before:
http://www.thestar.com/NASApp/cs/ContentServer?pagename=thestar/Render&inifile=futuretense.ini&c=Page&cid=990761496952&pubid=968163964505

After:
http://makeashorterlink.com/?I3E723982
http://tinyurl.com/laxs

STORY: As I stated with Wanda, women like Audrey are truly the Contest Queens of this fun and exciting hobby we all share. Audrey was lucky enough to "win" life long friends!

ଽୠଡ଼

Audrey—Grand Prairie, AB
Since 1991, I have amassed over $304,000 in prizes including over 25 trips (two to Paris, three to Florida, Germany (took the cash instead, $10,000!), Las Vegas, California more times than I can count, New York, Club Med Cancun...the list goes on and on. I have won three vehicles, two large screen TVs plus at least five others over 33" etc. etc. Just today I had a message on my answering machine that I won a complete set of stainless steel cookware.

In 1991 I won a Caribbean cruise through a contest with our local newspaper. While on the cruise, my husband and I met a very nice couple from California, Barry and Debbie, who were our dinner companions throughout the trip. We got along famously and found that we had a lot in common. Somehow the topic of contesting came up and Debbie joked, "Well, you will just have to win a trip to California so you can come to visit us."

Well, sure enough about one month after the cruise, I won not one, but two trips to California! We went down for a week, visited with them, then came down a week later, with a trip that originated in San Francisco and gave us a rental car to drive down the Pacific Coast Highway to Disneyland.

A few months after that, I won a trip to Florida. I immediately phoned up Debbie and asked if they would like to meet up with us there. They did, and we had a great time. We also won a ski trip for four to Lake Louise, and they flew up to join us. We even stayed in the famous Chateau Lake Louise!

We met again on another win, Club Med in Cancun, as well as several other trips that I won to California. We remain great friends and can't wait to see where we will win a trip to next so that we can meet up with them again!

80C8

Increasing Your Chances

There are many things you can do to increase your chances of winning. The first being **enter as often** as you can. Read the rules to determine what the entry parameters are: once per household, one time per person, daily, weekly, etc. The entry rules will determine how you proceed. This is especially important if a contest is labeled "per person" because you can then increase your chances by entering your family and friends.

TIP: Have a contesting circle of friends - it comes in handy when there are contests that will grant you bonus entries into the contest for referring other people. I have a standard list of ten friends that I use.

NOTE: Many contests ask for referrals without granting bonus entries. I only enter friend's email addresses in those contest that grant extra entries. I also only refer the friends I know will enter. Making friends in the contesting online communities can help because you know they will enter and increase your odds of winning. (see Join an Online Community.)

Entering as often as you can goes hand-in-hand with **entering over the entire contest entry period**. It is especially important to *stagger* your entries over the entire entry period when entering via regular mail because it may be financially prohibitive to mail in entries every day. (see *Staggering & Flooding*.)

Look for contests with **short entry periods**. Contests that are only open to accepting entries for a two week period will get far fewer entries than ones that are open for several months.

Promotions with **entry limitations** attract fewer entrants. I have seen contests limit entries to a city, an area code, a province and even specific age ranges.

Look for contests that offer **many prizes** as opposed to, or in conjunction with, a grand prize. We have won many terrific secondary prizes, and the odds of winning something are higher for the smaller prizes.

Some contests **take time to enter**. Any contest with qualifiers, specifically mail-in, such as hand-written essays or UPCs and HDFs, will draw fewer entrants.

TIP: Remember, it only takes one to win!

STORY: This story of how against all odds, in a daily entry contest, Mary only entered once and WON!

ॐ

Mary—St. Albert, AB
I couldn't believe my husband and I were going to the Pro Bowl in Hawaii and staying at the Village Hilton! I just wanted to let folks know that even though this contest could be entered once per day over a four month period, I only entered <u>ONCE</u>. So there you go—keep entering everyone. It only takes one entry. I was also told by the prize authorities the number of entries was approximately 61,000. So, this one was a 1 in 61,000 win.

ॐ

95

Time Saving Tips

There are many little things you can do that will save you time entering online:

1. Use the fastest computer you can.
2. Use the fastest Internet connection you can.
3. Use a mouse with a side button you can program to go back to the previous webpage when clicked (with your thumb).
4. Use contesting software packages such as RoboForm and/or Turbo Sweeps.
5. Have two IE windows open at once (or tabs in Firefox) and toggle back and forth between them. This is particularly handy when web pages are slow to load.
6. Only enter contests with prizes you really want to win. It takes as much time to win a car as it does movie passes.
7. Only enter the people that will share the prize with you, such as your spouse, child, or best friend.
8. Only enter the required fields. They are usually flagged by a * or are **bolded** or coloured.
9. Only enter online. Mail-in contests take quite a bit of time to enter in comparison to online promotions.

"You can't lose helping others win."
Anonymous

JOIN AN ONLINE COMMUNITY

Joining an online community is the best way to increase the number of contests you enter. Being a member of various online communities has also led me to several face to face meetings and making real friends. I feel posting contests and answers has helped me win because it follows the adage *you reap what you sow*. (see *Attracting Luck*.)

Contestors may also post when they will be visiting another city on holiday or a business trip. Fellow contestors will then meet them for a drink at the airport (on a stopover), for lunch, or take them on a tour of their city. It's great fun putting faces to the names you see online. I have had the pleasure of meeting many fellow contestors this way.

You may notice that people participating in the group seem to follow the 80/20 rule. i.e. 80% of the contests are posted by 20% of the members. Some of the reasons the majority of people do not post contests are: 1) some members are just better at finding contests 2) sometimes someone will go to post a contest or answer and find that it has already been posted and 3) some members have more time to post contests and answers.

Not all members will participate in the group. I call those people "lurkers." They enjoy the hobby of contesting and they learn about all the new contests and sweepstakes from the active members of the group, but they do not give back by posting anything they find or post their winnings. It is impossible to know what percentage of a group are lurkers because you will never hear from them. Don't be a lurker. The enjoyment I get from this hobby is just not the thrill of winning but the joy I get from my contesting friends. I feel you will miss out on a fantastic part of this hobby if you lurk.

NOTE: Do not fear monitored forums or chat rooms. The monitoring is not designed to be "Big Brother," rather it is to prevent any type of online abuse and keeps the site safe and clean for it's participants.

NOTE: These are the current most active community sites on the internet. The Internet is a very "fluid" place and sites can come and go in a heartbeat. You may wish to do frequent searches to find new online communities and contest websites. Remember to check www.contestqueen.com for updated Internet contesting resources.

NOTE: You must be a member of Yahoo to join any Yahoo Group, but it's free to sign-up for Yahoo and the groups.

Canada-Contests
Group
http://groups.yahoo.com/group/canada-contests
Qué Banh began the group Canada-Contests in 2003 when Canadacontests, the group she was originally a member of and which was not moderated, was taken over by spammers. She hosts her own contests for members and has at least one offline event annually. Her group not only lists Canadian-based promotions but all contests, including US-based and worldwide contests that are open to Canadians.

Canada Sweeps
Group
http://groups.yahoo.com/group/canadasweeps
Pat Galarneau-Trithart began Canada Sweeps in 2001. She felt the people in a group she belonged to were making people afraid to post, since there was little in the way of "netiquette" amongst its members. (That group has since closed.) She felt there was a need for a group which would promote friendly interaction between sweepers and contesters regardless of their level of experience, so she started just such a group where the rules of netiquette are more closely followed. This makes for a pleasant, safe online place for members to participate in the hobby of contesting.

To encourage participation by all, every member must post one new contest per month, with the exception of July, August, and December, or they will be asked to leave the group. If you are going on vacation, sick leave, etc. you can send a note to Pat and go into No Mail mode, thus retaining your membership status.

Canadiannetstakes
Forum

www.canadiannetstakes.ca/index.php
The forum has been a part of the www.canadiannetstakes.ca website (owned by Promodem—see *Contest Management Companies.*) since 2004. Its purpose is twofold: the first is to allow contest enthusiasts a monitored forum in which to share their hobby, and second is to allow Promodem to build a dialogue and relationship with the contestants.

Canuck Cash
Forum

http://forum.canuckcash.ca/index.php
Dave Rossborough originally set-up this forum because at the time he felt there was not the level of interactivity between fellow contestors that he desired on other Canadian contesting websites. This forum is very simple with only a few areas to post in, making it easy to read topics and messages from everyone in the group. This site has a separate membership from the website.

Concours Exchangeboard
Forum

http://concours.exchangeboard.com/forum
NOTE: This forum is in French.
This forum is perfect for Quebec contestors to share contests, answers and chat about promotions that are only open to Quebec residents and the French versions of Canadian contests. You must become a member to use the full site. Membership is free.

Contest Canada Plus++
Group

http://groups.yahoo.com/group/CCanada
Another contesting group is Contest Canada Plus++. You must be referred by a member to join. I have included this group in case you

discovered it while searching the Internet and wondered why you could not become a member.

NOTE: I will <u>not</u> refer anyone to Contest Canada Plus++ due the volume of requests I receive.

Frugal Shopper
Forum

www.frugalshopper.ca/phpbb2/index.php
This forum was added to the Frugal Shopper site for members to chat about contests, freebies and sales. Membership is free.

Goldfish Legs
Forum

http://gfl-free.ca
Costa Caruso began www.goldfishlegs.ca in January 2000 as a comparison shopping site for Canadians. He has a very good sense of humor and the site is very tongue in cheek. There is even a site mascot, Juju The Fish. The site originally only posted deals; later freebies were added, and finally contests became part of the mix. Now the contest section of his site is the most popular.

I Can Win
Group

http://groups.yahoo.com/group/icanwin
I have been a member of icanwin shortly after I became serious about contesting. I must give credit to the group for helping me by posting contests, answers, UPCs and answers to my many questions as I went from beginner to advanced contestor. (I hope through my own many posts I have given back to the group as much as I received.) I would not have been able to enter as many contests as I have without the group, and the basis of my system started here.

TIP: If there is an option, receive the group messages in digest form. They can be scanned through quite quickly. Also, potentially receiving hundreds of emails daily from "strangers" can be quite overwhelming. If you do choose to receive the groups in individual emails, set your email client up to move email from the group into a separate folder so it is automatically segregated from your personal and business correspondence.

> *"Play fair. Don't hit people.*
> *Say you're sorry when you hurt somebody."*
> *Robert Fulghum*

Contesting Etiquette

This section could also be called common sense. It is "Do unto others as you would have others do unto you." Since this book's focus is primarily on Internet contesting, the etiquette will focus primarily on how to behave within an online community, group or forum.

1) Post complete messages. Before clicking the Send button, review your message to ensure all relevant contest information is included. You should type a meaningful subject and then include a direct link to the contest and possibly the rules, what the prize is, eligibility, how many times one can enter and the end date of the contest.

EXAMPLE:
NC @ Contest Queen
http://www.contestqueen.com
win a car—open to all of Canada—one entry per person per day—
ends Dec 31st
GOOD LUCK,
Carolyn
in Oshawa

TIP: Always include the full URL including the http:// to make the link clickable in the message. Otherwise, one must copy or retype the link in a new window.

2) Keep your signature file to a reasonable length (4 to 7 lines is usually considered OK). It can be irritating for people to see the same huge signature over and over again.

3) If you post a message and it doesn't appear immediately, please be patient. The Internet is not always instant. I have seen the same message posted three and four times because someone didn't give the server a chance to process the original message.

4) DO NOT TYPE YOUR MESSAGE ALL IN CAPITALS. Not only is it hard to read, it is usually interpreted as shouting. If you can't use the shift key easily, all lowercase is much easier on the eyes and less likely to be misinterpreted.

5) Most groups and forums will not allow you to send attachments. This is to prevent viruses, pornography, and other unpleasantness from being proliferating to group members, and as a courtesy to members who have slow internet connections.

6) Do not forward other's postings or messages outside the group without getting permission from the author first. It is rude and inconsiderate, and posting a contest you didn't originally find to another group is disrespectful to both the group and the poster.

As a follow up to this, if you do need to forward information to a group (or to individuals, for that matter), delete any email addresses from the original message before you send. This is a simple courtesy—you wouldn't give out an acquaintance's phone number or home address without their permission, so don't give out their email address either.

NOTE: I post contests to many groups. However, I only post contests that I find myself. If another group member found it, I do not cross-post.

7) Post a Thank You to the group, naming the original poster, when you win something big. People like to be appreciated and to see their efforts of finding contests are indeed helping others win. It does make a difference.

8) Online groups and forums are not chat rooms. Do not send one-lined emails, such as "Thank you" or "Good idea". These types of messages should be avoided. When you send a message to the entire group you are potentially sending it to hundreds of people. If an email is intended

to be read by one particular person, then email that person directly. (Most people show their direct email address either in their message header or signature.)

9) Before you reply to a posting, think about whether or not the entire group needs to see your reply. If your posting is of a personal nature or directed to one person, email them directly.

10) If you are unsure if your email address is available for others to use when they want to send you a private message, you can put it in your signature file.

11) Remove all text that you are not replying too, including headers and signature lines. Extra text makes it difficult to read the reply. Trim quoted text down to just those points you are responding to. Generally, there should be more new text than quoted text. It can be very irritating to read the same message, quoted in its entirety, in dozens of replies. You can assume others have already read the post you are responding to. Remember, you should retain enough of the original message to maintain the context of the topic.

12) Read ALL emails before replying to one. A subject quickly becomes a "dead horse" when people do not do this.

13) If you are posting a message that is off topic, please mark the subject line with either the words Off Topic or the letters OT.

14) When entering a contest that asks for referrals, do not refer anyone without their permission first.

Etiquette altered and reprinted with permission from D'Arcy Emery.

TIP: For more family friendly Internet etiquette and cyber safety tips you can go to: http://disney.go.com/cybersafety or search the internet using the word "netiquette.".

"A snake lurks in the grass."
Virgil

SPYWARE, VIRUSES AND SPAM, OH MY!

One of the biggest concerns or reservations that people tell me they have about entering contests and sweepstakes on the Internet is the possible dangers. They always ask if I get a lot of spam or viruses from entering online. These are certainly valid concerns with some of the nasty computer viruses and spyware running around on the Internet. When you get into the mode of doing a lot of Internet-based contesting, you simply need to be aware of these hazards and ensure that you have the proper tools running on your machine to keep them out of your computer.

TIP: You should safeguard all your computers against spyware, viruses, spam, etc. regardless of if you are entering online contests or not. PERIOD. If you are on the Internet, any unprotected computer is vulnerable to these hazards.

Terminology

Here are some basic definitions of terms that you should be familiar with when reading through this section:

Active X Controls

Active X is technology produced by Microsoft that enables different applications to interact easily with each other. For example, Microsoft Word can be opened in an Internet Explorer browser and specific communications needs to occur between Microsoft Word & Internet Explorer. Sometimes these communication rules are exploited by malicious applications and they can cause harm to your computer.

Browser Hijackers/Browser Helper Objects (BHO)

Browser hijackers are programs that run automatically every time you start your internet browser. These hijackers can sometimes control your browser, like Internet Explorer. Some Browser Helper Objects are really good for expanding your browser capabilities, but there are others that may not need your permission to install and which can be used for malicious purposes like gathering information on your surfing habits. This can cause anything from incompatibility issues to corrupting important system functions, making them not only a threat to your security, but also to your systems stability.

Data Mining

Data mining is an information extraction activity whose goal is to discover hidden facts contained in databases. Using a combination of machine learning, statistical analysis, modeling techniques, and database technology, data mining finds patterns and subtle relationships in data and infers rules that allow the prediction of future results. For example: people purchasing wood on the Internet would have painting supplies cross sold to them. Typical applications include market segmentation, customer profiling, fraud detection, evaluation of retail promotions, and credit risk analysis.

Drive-by Downloads

A drive-by download is a program that is automatically downloaded to your computer, often without your consent or even your knowledge. Unlike a pop-up download, which asks for consent (albeit in a deceitful manner likely to lead to a "yes"), a drive-by download is carried out invisibly to the user. They can be initiated by simply visiting a Web site or viewing an HTML email message. Frequently, a drive-by download is installed along with another application.

Keyloggers

Keyloggers are programs that capture and record your every keystroke, including personal information and passwords. They are designed to monitor computer activity to various degrees. These programs can capture virtually everything you do on your computer, including recording of all keystrokes, emails, chat room dialogue, web sites visited, and programs run. System monitors usually run in the background so that you do not know you are being monitored. The information gathered by the system monitor is stored on your computer in an encrypted log file for later retrieval. Some programs are even capable of emailing the log files to another location.

Parasites

Parasites are programs that get installed on your computer, which you never asked for, and do some type of activity that you didn't intend for it to do. Almost all the parasites that are currently known are only compatible with Windows, and some only affect the Internet Explorer browser.

Registry Keys

Microsoft Windows stores all of your application information in your registry keys, for example, what software to run, where is the software located, etc. Viruses can manipulate these settings so that applications stop running or run when least expected.

Scumware

Scumware often alters the content of web sites you are accessing, changing the normal links to re-route you to other web sites. They can also broadcast information that you submit in forms, create more pop-up windows in your browser, and track each and every web site that you visit, how long you stay, and which links you clicked on. Most of the time scumware hides itself on your computer in multiple locations to hinder the removal process.

Toolbars

Toolbars can be downloaded to your web browser to make browsing easier. Examples are the Google, Alexa, and Yahoo toolbars. Even though these toolbars are very handy to use, they have the ability to track everything you do on the Internet and then pass that information back to the owners of the toolbars. Be sure to read the terms and conditions page before you download any toolbar.

Tracking Cookies

Cookies are small pieces of information that are generated by a web server and stored on your computer for future access. Cookies were originally implemented to allow you to customize your web experience, and still continue to serve useful purposes in enabling a personalized web experience. However, some web sites now issue adware cookies, which allow multiple web sites to store and access cookies that may contain personal information (including surfing habits, user names and passwords, areas of interest, etc.), and then simultaneously share the information they contain with other web sites. This sharing of information allows marketing firms to create a user profile based on your personal information and sells it to other firms. Adware cookies are almost always installed and accessed without your knowledge or consent.

NOTE: Some websites that host contests on a regular basis use cookies so that when a frequent user returns it is very easy for them to enter a new promotion. www.muchmusic.com/contests is a good example of a site that uses cookies. If you are using one computer to enter multiple people (family and friends), then you will need to clear the cookies before entering each person. In Internet Explorer this can be done by clicking on TOOLS, INTERNET OPTIONS and DELETE COOKIES.

Trojans
Trojans are malicious programs that appear as harmless or desirable applications. Trojans are designed to cause loss or theft of computer data, and to destroy your system. Some trojans, called RATs (Remote Administration Tools), allow an attacker to gain unrestricted access of your computer whenever you are online. The attacker can perform activities such as file transfers, adding/deleting files or programs, and controlling the mouse and keyboard. Trojans are generally distributed as email attachments or bundled with another software program.

Spyware and Adware
Spyware is any technology or application on your computer that covertly gathers personal information, computer activity or computer content and sends this information to a third party. The data is then sold to advertisers or to other interested parties. The type of information harvested from your computer varies. Some spyware tracks your system information only, such as your type of Internet connection and type of operating system. Other spyware collects personal information,

such as detailed tracking of your Internet surfing habits, or worse, the harvesting of your personal files.

Spyware is installed without the user's consent (if you give consent for a company to collect your data this is no longer considered spying, so read online data disclosure statements carefully before consenting). Some people don't object to general spying that track Internet and software trends as long as personal identifying information is not included; others object to any information being taken from their computer without their consent. Either way, the software or device that gathers the information is called spyware.

Adware is considered to go beyond the reasonable advertising that one might expect from freeware or shareware. Typically a separate program that is installed at the same time as a shareware or similar program, Adware will usually continue to generate advertising even when the user is not running the originally desired program. A good example of Adware was a series of products released by Gator, which would just pop-up an installer when you visited certain web sites or pages. The installer would offer you a generally useful utility such as a tool to synchronize your computer clock with an internet time source; a great tool for those who are not running Windows XP, which already includes this feature. However along with the time sync tool also came a piece of code that allowed Gator to push pop-up ads to your computer. It would also be installed as a separate application from the time sync tool, so you would have to know what the pop-up application was called to completely uninstall it.

Adware/Spyware can also simply take the form of web site cookies that are left on your machine for tracking purposes. Other sites will see these tracking cookies and know about the other sites that you have visited.

Keep in mind that you may not always get a pop-up or any indication that these applications or cookies are being installed on your computer. Malicious coders are taking advantage of the many security holes that exist in Microsoft's various Windows operating systems and especially in the Microsoft Internet Explorer browser. Many alternative browsers specifically do not support Microsoft's ActiveX and VB Script technologies due to the number of security issues associated with them.

There are a lot of products available now to help you monitor and combat Spyware and Adware on your computer. There are tools that you pay for and free tools that can be installed on your computer, or there are also web sites that offer free scanners that you can visit periodically to check your machine. In cases where you are a regular web surfer, it is recommended to have an installed tool on your machine that will proactively check what is happening on your computer and block some of the nastier versions of these applications from getting on your machine in the first place.

NOTE: These tools work much like anti-virus tools and have signature files of known Spyware and Adware technologies. These files need to be updated regularly to combat recent releases of Spyware and Adware on the Internet. Usually these tools have a built-in feature to go and check for product updates.

Anti-Spyware/Adware Tools

While there are dozens of tools available and we recommend that you find a tool that you are comfortable using, we will highlight some of the more popular tools being used below to help get you started:

Spy Sweeper

Spy Sweeper boasts an extensive, easy-to-understand feature set. While scanning for spy or ad components, you can view a progress bar and timer to gauge how long the scanning process is going to take. This product also comes with prevention features that will keep many spyware items from downloading in the first place instead of just removing the offending programs after the fact.

By default, Spy Sweeper starts up with Windows and runs in the background to prevent your computer from activating spyware. Spy Sweeper adds new criteria to its search capabilities frequently to ensure that it finds the most recent spyware programs. When a spyware component is found, Spy Sweeper provides a brief description and severity analysis then asks you if you want to quarantine the offending object, where you can delete it. The spyware components found are listed in a tree-like diagram separated into categories that allow you easy, organized inspection. Spy Sweeper even offers a rollback feature that will allow you to restore deleted or quarantined components if you change your mind. The "More Details" button will send you to a website that provides further information on most spyware.

Available from: Webroot Software Inc.
www.webroot.com
Cost: $29.95 USD
Free trial version is also available for download.

Spyware Eliminator

Like many other spyware removers, Spyware Eliminator has the ability to rollback your decisions after deleting spyware—you can change your mind and put that cookie back. Also, the program gives a color-coded severity graph for each spyware component found. When you click on an uncovered spyware program you can read a more detailed explanation of its content. Spyware Eliminator also protects your Internet browser from spyware that would attempt to change your Internet settings.

Available from: Aluria Software
www.aluriasoftware.com
Cost: $29.95 USD
Also offer a free scanner for download.

Ad-Aware

Ad-Aware is one of the older and better known anti-spyware packages. One unique add-on to Ad-Aware Professional is a built-in popup blocker. This is a wonderful addition for those that would otherwise go out and purchase a blocker. The software also comes with Ad-watch—Lavasoft's answer to real-time monitoring. Ad-Aware will monitor your Internet activity and warn you if your computer attempts to download spyware or adware; you have the preemptive option to cancel the installation. In addition, you can block ActiveX and web installations to minimize the risk of downloading spyware. It also provides rollback capabilities so you can restore components you may want to keep (deleting some components may disable some desired applications that are dependent on adware). Ad-Aware also comes in three different flavours with increasing features and capabilities. The standard version is free and gives you the basic capability of scanning your system and removing suspected problems.

Available from: Lavasoft
www.lavasoft.us
Cost: Standard: Free; Plus: $26.95 USD; Professional: $39.95 USD

SpyBot Search & Destroy
Spybot - Search & Destroy can detect and remove spyware of different kinds from your computer. Spyware is a relatively new kind of threat that common anti-virus applications do not yet cover. If you see new toolbars in your Internet Explorer that you didn't intentionally install, if your browser crashes, or if you browser start page has changed without your knowing, you most probably have spyware. But even if you don't see anything, you may be infected, because more and more spyware is emerging that is silently tracking your surfing behaviour to create a marketing profile of you that will be sold to advertisement companies.

Available from: Safer Networking
www.safer-networking.org/index.php?page=spybotsd
Cost: Free

Free Web-Based Scanners
Both Webroot Software and Aluria software offer a web-based scanning option for free which can be found here:

Webroot—Spy Audit
www.webroot.com/services/spyaudit_03.htm?rc=612

Aluria—Spyware Scan
www.aluriaaffiliates.com/go.rd?id=22a8x1232c3752

Malware
Malware is short for MALicious softWARE. It is a generic term increasingly being used to describe any form of malicious software; e.g., viruses, worms, trojan horses, malicious active content, etc.

The first form of Malware to evolve was the computer virus. Viruses work and spread (within the infected system) by attaching themselves to other pieces of software (or in the case of macro viruses, documents and spreadsheets), such that during the execution of the program the viral code is executed. Viruses spread across computers when the software or document they are attached to is transferred from one computer to the other.

Computer worms are similar to viruses but are stand-alone software and thus do not require other pieces of software to attach themselves to. They do modify their host operating system, however, at least to the extent that they are started as part of the boot process. To spread, worms either exploit some vulnerability of the target system or use some kind of social engineering to trick users into executing them (such as an enticing e-mail attachment).

Trojan horses are similar to viruses in that they get executed by being part of an otherwise useful piece of software. However, Trojan horses must be attached to the host software manually, and can not infect other pieces of software the way viruses can. To spread, Trojan horses rely on the useful features of the host software, which trick users into installing them.

A backdoor is a piece of software that allows access to the computer system bypassing the normal authentication procedures. Based on how they work and spread there are two groups of backdoors. The first group works much like a Trojan, i.e., they are manually inserted into another piece of software, executed via their host software, and spread by their host software being installed. The second group works more like a worm in that they get executed as part of the boot process and are usually spread by worms carrying them as their payload.

Anti-virus products are the most common products used to fight Malware. These products are quite mature and have compiled many years of experience in finding and fighting viruses worms and trojans on your computer. There are two types of anti-virus scans: active and passive. In an active scan, the system monitors and scans the files you use, e-mails you read and web sites you visit for the existence of a virus or worm. It will then block it from entering your system. A passive scanner is simply a scheduled scan of your system on a daily or weekly basis and does not protect you while you are using the system. Your anti-virus product should have both passive and active capabilities.

Anti-virus/Malware Tools

There are literally hundreds of tools all over the net that provides anti-virus features. We will include some of the more popular tools that are widely used and available.

PC-cillin

PC-cillin anti-virus protection features an integrated firewall, a WebTrap that blocks malicious Java and ActiveX programs, a MacroTrap that monitors Excel and Word files for viruses, and a Site Filter that allows you to block access to specific web sites.
For email, PC-cillin scans both POP3 accounts and Webmail. PC-cillin automatically cleans infected files, but if a file can't be cleaned, the software will place the file in quarantine. You can configure PC-cillin to prompt you every time an infected file is discovered so you can immediately consider your options.

PC-cillin also provides mobile users the extra protection needed to stay virus-free on the road, including Wi-Fi (Wireless Fidelity) connection security for your wireless protection and PDA (Personal Digital Assistant) synchronization protection.

Available from: Trend Micro Inc.
www.trendmicro.com
Cost: $39.95 USD

NOD32 Antivirus

NOD32 Antivirus System provides well balanced, state-of-the-art protection against threats endangering your PC and enterprise systems running various platforms from Microsoft Windows 95/98/ME/NT/2000/2003/XP, through a number of UNIX/Linux, Novell, MS DOS operating systems to Microsoft Exchange Server, Lotus Domino and other mail servers.

Viruses, worms, trojans and other malware are kept out of striking distance of your valuable data. Advanced detection methods implemented in the software even provide protection against the future threats from most of the new worms and viruses.

The fourth generation of the NOD32 Antivirus System features a fully integrated software suite characterized by an unprecedented detection track record, the fastest scanning rates and extremely low utilization of system resources.

Available from: Eset Inc.
www.nod32.com/products
Cost: $39.00 USD for initial purchase, $27.00 per year for updates after first year.

Bit Defender
The Live! Update feature checks for product and virus definition updates at either a user-defined interval or manually (default is every eight hours). When you do a manual check for updates, you decide which updates to install. When the software automatically checks for updates, it can update the files at that time or at a time you previously specified during setup.

BitDefender Standard Edition uses the ICSA Labs certified scanning engines, allowing users to feel secure about their virus protection. A very large folder (1.5 gigabyte with over 12,000 files) only took approximately 10 minutes to scan.

Available From: SoftWIN
www.bitdefender.com/index.php
Cost: $29.95 USD

NOTE: Anti-virus/Malware tools rely on signature files that get updated frequently by vendors to be able to keep up with new and changing virus strains that are being released. You should keep your signature files up to date to ensure that your computer is protected. Many of these products have a feature to automatically check for updates. This feature should always be enabled and check for updates daily.

Spam

Spam is flooding the internet with many copies of the same message, in an attempt to force the message on people who would not otherwise choose to receive it. Most spam is commercial advertising, often for dubious products, get-rich-quick schemes, or quasi-legal services. Spam costs very little to send—most of the costs are paid for by the recipient or the carriers rather than by the sender.

Email Spam targets individual users with direct mail messages. Spam lists are often created by scanning usenet postings, stealing internet mailing lists, or searching the web for addresses. Email spams typically cost users money out-of-pocket to receive. Many people—anyone with measured phone service—read or receive their mail while the meter is running, so to speak. Spam costs them additional money. On top of that, it costs money for ISPs and online services to transmit spam, and these costs are transmitted directly to subscribers.

One particularly nasty variant of email spam is sending spam to mailing lists (public or private email discussion forums). Because many mailing lists limit activity to their subscribers, spammers will use automated tools to subscribe to as many mailing lists as possible, so that they can grab the lists of addresses, or use the mailing list as a direct target for their attacks.

Contests usually work as a marketing tool and try to include getting your e-mail address. Many of the contesting forms that you fill-in will include check-boxes to include or exclude yourself from e-mails being sent to you outside of the purposes of the contest. You should be vigilant at ensuring that you are excluded from any of these mailing lists to cut down on your exposure to Spam. There are still other ways and other sources for marketers to figure out e-mail addresses, so anti-spam software is highly recommended to keep the volumes manageable. (see *Opt-In or Opt-Out?*)

Anti-Spam tools

There is a wide range of anti-spam tools available, and many of them work different ways to eliminate spam from costing you time and effort in your inbox. Below I will give you a few examples of some of the different styles of spam blocking. It is up to you to figure our which tool works best for your needs.

Be sure to look at the support requirements on the products. If you are using a web-mail box on a large service like Yahoo or MSN, they have spam blocking tools available that you can add to your mail account. For those that use a traditional ISP e-mail account that downloads to your computer from a POP3 source, then you need to match an anti-spam tool to software you use to read your e-mail (e.g. Outlook Express, Eudora, Netscape or Thunderbird).

MailWasher

MailWasher lets you make a spammer think that your e-mail address is invalid. You can also choose to delete a message on your e-mail server, without downloading it. MailWasher retrieves information about all e-mail messages on the server.

To check e-mail, you don't open your e-mail client. Instead, you start MailWasher, and it tells you what messages are waiting for you on the mail server. In the check boxes, you select whether to Delete or Bounce messages, then click the Process Mail button. If you have checked nothing, the e-mail is downloaded to your e-mail client as normal. You can also tell MailWasher to add e-mail addresses to your "friends" list or to your "blacklist"—this will tell MailWasher to always consider the address safe if it is on your friends list or spam if it is on your blacklist. MailWasher will attempt to recognize whether e-mails are safe or spam based on their similarity to messages that have be processed in the past.

Available from: MailWasher
www.mailwasher.net
Cost: Standard: Free; Pro: $37.00 USD

SpamNet

This product integrates with either Outlook or Outlook Express, and gives you access to a community of over one million Spam fighters. Install in minutes and forget about it. SpamNet starts working immediately without any configuration or hassle. Every time you block a spam message that slips through, your vote benefits the entire community. Typically dozens of people will vote a spam message as spam long before you go to download it, so this tool can be very effective at keep spam from hitting your Inbox. Can be configured to automatically delete spam, or quarantine it for your review in case a good message gets caught. You can unblock and white-list addresses of newsletters and mass mailings that you want to make sure you receive.

Available from: Cloudmark
www.cloudmark.com/products/spamnet
Cost: $39.95 USD per year.

SpamCombat

SpamCombat uses a powerful set of filter rules to prevent spam from entering your inbox: Whitelist, Blacklist, HTML Validator, DNSBL filter, and the Bayesian filters. The Whitelist and Blacklist are the standard lists where you can add conditions to automatically mark an email as good or spam. The messages can be whitelisted/blacklisted based on any words from the message header and/or body, and on the sender's IP address. SpamCombat is provided with a solid Blacklist, which allows you to catch the most known kinds of spam and virus emails. The DNSBL filter consists of comparing the senders' IP addresses against lists of known spam databases using Public Blacklists (also called DNSBL lists). These databases are maintained and updated daily. The Bayesian filter is the most powerful Spam filter based on the analysis of the message content and mathematical calculation of Spam. The advantage of the Bayesian filter is that the filter can be trained by each individual user by categorizing each received email as either spam or good; after you categorized a few emails the filter begins making this categorization by itself. If the filter makes a mistake, you re-categorize the email; the filter learns from its mistakes. The accuracy of the Bayesian filter increases with time. A "well trained" filter can determine up to 99.5% of spam emails coming into your inbox.

Available from: G-lock Software
www.glocksoft.com/sc/index.htm
Cost: Free (single mail account only); or $29.95 USD for multiple mail accounts.

Pop-Ups

Another annoying technology when surfing the Internet is Pop-Ups, Pop-Overs, Pop-Unders and various other advertising techniques that throw extra browser windows at you for things you probably aren't interested in. This technology is thankfully starting to fade. Most web browsers and common browser add-ons now include pop-up blocking features. Some of the products that we mention above include pop-up blockers. Yahoo and Google offer Microsoft Internet Explorer add-on Toolbars that provide pop-up blocking as a feature. You should enable this feature to prevent pop-ups on your system.

TIP: Some contesting sites may rely on the pop-up technology to be operational on your browser. If you are clicking on something over and over without any results, try turning the pop-up blocker off and clicking again. Remember to re-enable your pop-up blocker after you have finished with that web site. Some more advanced pop-up blockers will allow you to create a list of sites where you want pop-ups enabled, this can eliminate the need to remember where to turn the blocking capabilities on and off. Also, many pop-up blockers can be bypassed with a keyboard combination, allowing you to open pop-ups on a case by case basis.

"I've found that luck is quite predictable.
If you want more luck, take more chances.
Be more active. Show up more often."
Brian Tracy

YOU'RE A WINNER!!

You will be notified of a win by one of the following methods: by telephone, email, courier, or mail. Most of my contest win notifications have been by phone. I get notified via mail and email almost evenly, and I have only had a handful of couriered notifications. **(Sometimes, prizes just arrive in the mail. I love those!!)**

TIP: Keep a small note pad, pen and calculator by every phone in the house (even with your cell phone) in case you are called. I have interviewed many people that lost out on prizes because they were not prepared!

The Call

The person calling will ask for the potential winner, introduce themselves and their company, usually mention the contest name (e.g. Escape to Paradise Contest) and depending on the value of the prize along with what was required on the entry form, possibly a STQ (Skill Testing Question).

Write down all pertinent information regarding the caller: get the caller's name, company name and phone number. This is important because if you need to contact the contest management company or the sponsor regarding the contest, rules, release forms or the prize you know where to begin.

I was driving in my car and I took a winning notification call on my cell. Obviously, I was not able to write down the name and number of the person I spoke with. Murphy's Law was hard at work on that win. I keep a spreadsheet of all my wins (see sample below) and I know when a prize has taken longer than the standard 6-8 weeks (usually after the end-date of the promotion) to arrive. The only thing I knew was who the contest sponsor was, so I began there. It took me two weeks to finally speak to the contest management company. It took a total of sixteen weeks for my prize to arrive. What I do now is let the person know I am driving and I ask them to call me back at an appropriate time.

Winner	Date	Prize	Where	Value
		CONTESTING WINS 2005		
Carolyn	11-Jan	Dairy Queen Gift Certificates	New VR	$20.00
Carolyn	11-Jan	Shiseido Hair Care Sample	Flare	$2.50
Craig	17-Jan	Metro Home Show Tickets & Olay Gift Basket	680 NEWS	$124.00
Carolyn	18-Jan	Vikings T-Shirt & Baseball Cap	canada.com	$25.00
Carolyn	19-Jan	Two Nights at a Bed & Breakfast of our Choice	Smucker's	$300.00
Carolyn	31-Jan	Two Tickets to SUM 41 @ The Docks	Rogers	$60.00
			JANUARY TOTAL	$531.50
Carolyn	1-Feb	Four CHFI Coffee Mugs	CHFI 98.1	$24.00
Carolyn	2-Feb	HP Home Photo Lab	Country 95 3	$800.00
Tom	4-Feb	Culinary Gift Basket	Hellmann's	$80.00
Carolyn	8-Feb	One Song Music Download	L'Oreal	$0.99
Carolyn	8-Feb	Yves Rocher Gift Basket	Reader's Digest	$280.00
Tom	15-Feb	Four Passes to the Toronto Autoshow	CHFI 98.1	$80.00
Carolyn	16-Feb	Two Passes to see Michael Buble @ CityTV	CHUM FM	$30.00
Craig	17-Feb	$18.50	50/50 Draw @ Bowling	$18.50
Carolyn	22-Feb	Romantic Weekend Getaway for Two to Quebec	CTV	$500.00
Craig	24-Feb	$19.50	50/50 Draw @ Bowling	$19.50
Carolyn	25-Feb	Polly Pocket Toy Prize	Family Channel	$55.00
Craig	27-Feb	One Song Music Download	L'Oreal	$0.99
Craig	28-Feb	Family Pass to the Ontario Science Centre	Toronto 4 Kids	$70.00
			FEBRUARY TOTAL	$1,918.98
Craig	8-Mar	49ers Reebok Football Jersey	canada.com	$100.00
Carolyn	10-Mar	Movie Passes - Beauty Shop	FLOW 93.5	$26.00
Craig	10-Mar	Movie Passes - Beauty Shop	FLOW 93.5	$26.00
Craig	30-Mar	Green Bay Packers Football	canada.com	$35.00
Carolyn	31-Mar	Hockey Hall of Fame Keychain	Kraft	$2.95
			MARCH TOTAL	$189.95

TIP: If you are not ready to answer the STQ because you are driving, your kids are screaming, you're too nervous and want to calm down, etc., ask them to call you back and give them an appropriate time. If possible, also get their name and number.

If you are entering others that live in the same household and they are not available at the time "the call" comes in, take a message for the potential winner, again ensuring you write down all the pertinent information. If no one is home, a voicemail message is usually left. However, I have seen contest rules state that if they cannot reach a potential winner, they will not leave a message and another name will be drawn.

Depending on the contest rules you will either be sent your prize directly or you may have to sign and send back release forms before you are able to claim your prize.

The Letter

Letters arrive either via Canada Post in your regular mail, by registered mail, or via a courier such as FedEx, Purolator, or UPS. The notification usually includes a congratulatory letter along with all the release forms. You are generally given a few methods to send back the forms: mail, fax, email (after you scan the forms) or by courier. Since we run our business from home, I usually fax them back due to the ease and speed of returning the forms.

The Email

I have only received one email notifying me of a large win. All my other email notifications are for smaller prizes such as movie passes, CDs, books, etc. Many people are wary of opening emails stating they have won something due to past experience with fraudulent correspondence. (see *Scams*.) A legitimate email will be similar to a phone call. It will contain the contest name, possibly what you have won, potentially a STQ, the company name (of either the sponsor or the management company) and who to contact. You will usually be asked to respond/reply to the email within a specified period of time to claim your prize. Most people do remember what promotions they have entered, recognize the contest name and will know if it is a legitimate email. If you are unsure, call the contact at the bottom of the email.

You Win Some, You Lose Some

I wanted to include a different type of story in this book. A story of great excitement, anticipation, disappointment and finally hope.

I received an email stating I was a Grand Prize Contestant in the Coca-Cola® Mac's iCoke.ca/winamini Contest. At first I thought I won a Mini. I called Craig up from his office to read the email to determine what I had really won while I stopped hyperventilating. What 'Grand Prize Contestant' meant, was, I was one of a hundred chosen for the opportunity to go to Paramount Canada's Wonderland (an amusement park north of Toronto) on the following Saturday and participate in a key-turn draw for a chance to win a 2005 Mini Cooper Classic. 1 in 100 odds of winning a car were really good!!

I use, on a regular basis, all the techniques I talk about in the Attracting Luck chapter. Now, all I seemed to do 24/7 was meditate, think or dream about winning the Mini. I went down to the local Mini dealership, studied the key, took a test drive and bought a Mini t-shirt to wear at the draw. I even had my insurance company give me a quote.

The rules stated I was to arrive at the park three hours before the draw. Since Craig and Nicole came with me, we had time to wander the park, look at all the cool sights and have a bite to eat.

At the appointed time, we gathered at the showcase where the draw was being held. The Mini Cooper Classic was up on the stage surrounded by balloons and lit up with spot lights. (New cars can really shine!) The contest management company representative came out and gave us a brief overview of what was going to take place. There were sixty keys, each in a little box, on the display table. Wait…Only sixty?! It turns out that sixty out of the hundred potential car winners replied with the proper forms and actually showed up for the draw. My odds had just gotten much better!

They would draw a name from the drawing drum, that person would come up, select a box from the table, go to the car, get in the car and see if their key started the engine. If the key started the engine that person would win the car. Potentially, the drawing could end right away if the first person selected the winning key.

They drew the first name. Not me. The fellow went up, selected a box, and tried to start the car. No go. This went on for about ten more people. Then my name was called. My stomach dropped. My hands were shaking. My heart was racing. I somehow managed to make it to the stage without my knees buckling. I went up, shook hands with the sponsors, closed my eyes and prayed God would lead my hand to the right key.

I walked over to the car and got in. A representative from Coca-Cola was in the passenger seat ready to help the contestants. I put my foot on the clutch. (It was a standard car and the car would not start if the clutch was not depressed even if I had the right key.) I opened the little box and looked at the key. It didn't look like a Mini key. (Was the Classic key different from the standard Cooper and Cooper S keys??) I began to panic. The key wouldn't even go in to the ignition. The representative said she was sorry. If I couldn't get the key in the ignition it wasn't the right key. I didn't win the car.

I got out of the car and was asked to draw the name of the next contestant. I picked a name from the drum and then turned to go back to my seat. I was so sad, as I walked back to Craig and Nicole. I felt like the biggest loser. I really thought, with all my heart, I was going to win that car. I guess it wasn't meant to be.

We sat in the stands watching to see what would happen. Only about five more names were called before someone started the car. The entire process only lasted about 30 minutes. I realized I was lucky to even have a chance to go up and try because about two-thirds of the contestants didn't even get a chance to pick a key. Also, the young man that won the car didn't even own one. He needed the car more than I did.

I chose to include this particular story because I wanted you to know: 1) I do not win every contest I enter and 2) I continue to be happy and excited every day about entering contests, dreaming about the prizes I could win, being and feeling lucky, and just overall passionate about contesting.

Release Forms

It is important to read the documentation sent to you because you could lose if you do not respond correctly or within the specified period of time. Release forms are the legal release that you and any companions sign stating you agree to and will abide by the contest rules and regulations.

Once, I won a $100 gift certificate and while speaking with the contest management service representative, I discovered my name was the third one drawn. The first two "winners" did not call them back.

*NOTE: The time limit to respond will differ from contest to contest, so again, **read the rules** to determine how much time you have to reply. Otherwise, you may forfeit the prize.*

TIP: I have had winning notifications arrive by mail the day the release forms are due back at the management company or even several days after. Call them immediately, explain your predicament and you will generally get your prize. Everyone understands that postal mail sometimes takes much longer to arrive than originally anticipated.

STORY: Kevin is my husband's best friend and only entered this contest with Craig's encouragement. Unfortunately, Kevin won, and then lost because he was unable to respond within the specified period of time set out in the contest rules.

℘ℭ

Kevin—Markham, ON

I work for a Swiss company, and occasionally they need me to go to head office for extended periods of time. Craig saw a contest from a major software manufacturer that would pay the winner back the purchase price of any new computers that were bought with their applications installed. I rarely enter contests, but had recently purchased a new laptop. Craig encouraged me to enter, so I thought 'what the heck—a free laptop is very affordable...'

I was on a business trip in Switzerland and due to fly home when my employer asked me to stay an extra three weeks to work on a large project. As (un)luck would have it, the draw took place during those extra three weeks, my name was selected, and the contest company FedEx'd me the release forms. But no one was opening my mail while I was away, so no one in my home realized how important the package was. Two days before the forms were due back, the contest company left an urgent voice mail on my cellphone—but I also wasn't checking messages while I was away. I finally returned from overseas late on a Friday afternoon and got the messages—too late. It was after six o'clock, and I was unable to reach anyone at the contest company. At that point, I was so jetlagged and disgusted at the situation I didn't bother trying to contact them again.

And no, the extra three weeks at head office didn't pay back the cost of the laptop….

ಐ෬

TIP: If you plan to be away on vacation, to avoid losing out on a win, have a close relative or friend check your email, your voice mail and read your mail. You can check your voicemail yourself inexpensively using Canada Direct (www.infocanadadirect.com) and your calling card. You can check your email yourself by visiting internet cafés and using a web-based mail service (http://services.mail2web.com) or if you are taking your laptop you can seek out Wi-Fi "hotspots". (http://forbes.jiwire.com)

STQs

There is quite a debate amongst my fellow contestors regarding STQs (Skill Testing Questions). Are questions answered calculating left to right or should BEDMAS be used?

e.g. $8 + 2 \times 4$

left-to right = 40 (8 plus 2 equals 10, times 4 equals 40)

BEDMAS = 16 (multiplication always comes before addition, so 2 times 4 equals 8, plus 8 equals sixteen)

If you are using BEDMAS, operations are done in a specific order. This order is as follows:
1. Simplify all operations inside of parentheses (brackets).
2. Simplify all exponents, working your way from left to right.
3. Complete all multiplications and divisions, working your way from left to right.
4. Complete all additions and subtractions, working your way from left to right.

BEDMAS is defined as:
   B - Brackets
   E - Exponents

D - Division
M - Multiplication
A - Addition
S – Subtraction

A good STQ will be written in such a way that the answer will be the same either way or will be *written* out.

$2 \times 4 + 8 = 16$
or
Multiply 40 by 2
Add 10
Divide by 2
Subtract 5
Answer = 40

If you get an STQ and are unsure how to answer it, *ask*. If called, I will ask if the question is to be answered left-to-right or using BEDMAS. The sponsors and contest management companies want you to win so they will direct you on how to answer. Most times they will read out one set of operations before going on to the next one.

e.g. Please add 2 and 8. Now multiply by 4. Now minus 10. What's the answer? 10.

If I get mailed or emailed release forms and are unsure of which formula to use (left-to-right or BEDMAS), I put in both answers explaining why there are two answers. Maybe next time they will create a less confusing STQ. There usually aren't many math majors in the marketing department!

Why We Have Skill Testing Questions

In order to avoid being classified as an illegal lottery, you have to remove chance *or* consideration from your promotion. There are two ways to deal with the question of chance. The most straightforward is to eliminate chance altogether by conducting a pure skill contest. The other way to deal with the question of chance is by adding an element of skill to a random selection process.

Skill-testing Question:
All contests must have an element of skill. This requirement is inherently met by skill contests. Other contests satisfy this requirement with a mathematical question. Check with your lawyer before you use any other kind of skill. Canadian case law is quite bizarre on what constitutes sufficient skill. For example, identifying the characters in a sitcom or the products in a catalogue would probably not involve sufficient skill. Mathematical skill-testing questions should consist of a 4-part equation with 2 to 3 digit numbers which either follows the order of mathematics (x, ÷, +, -) or uses brackets. We do not know how difficult the math must be but Grade 6 level is probably not enough (unless the contest is aimed at children).

Reproduced with permission from LexisNexis Canada Inc., Pritchard & Vogt, Advertising and Marketing Law in Canada, 2004.

An interesting white paper on gaming, betting, STQs and NPEs in Canada written by Michael Lipton, can be found here: www.gaminglawmasters.com/jurisdictions/canada/SkillvsChanceOct2004.htm

NOTE: Sometimes the mathematical operators for multiplication (x) and divide (÷) are shown as a star (*) and a forward slash (/) respectively.

STORY: Fred submitted a very funny story about his wife Betty and her first experience with answering an over-the-phone Skill Testing Question.

ଚୀଘ

Fred—Prince George, BC
The wife got her first phone call and skill testing question today. It went something like this: Wife answers phone and runs into computer

room, "Fred I think I won something!" Then talks on the phone, "I had better sit down." CRASH! BANG! OUCH! Picks up phone while lying on floor and says, "I missed the chair." I pick up extension phone and hear a guy laughing so hard he can hardly say the skill testing question. The wife hollers, "Fred have you got the answer?" More laughing. Then she says, "My husband says it's 350." I hear some guy say, "I guess that is right, what is your email address?" Wife says "XXX funny sign XXX dot CA." I hear more laughing and the guy says, "Well you made my day! Did you hurt yourself? You have won an Apple iPod." Wife, "An I what?" "An iPod." says the guy. Wife, "Is that something to do with glasses?" Guy, "I wish I had this on tape." That's when I hung up the extension.

NOTE: Betty's email address was Xed out to protect her privacy.

৪৩৫৪

"Of course the game is rigged.
Don't let that stop you—if you
don't play, you can't win."
Robert Heinlein

SCAMS

YOU NEVER HAVE TO PAY TO RECEIVE A PRIZE FROM A LEGITIMATE CONTEST!!

I cannot stress this enough.

The only monies you may have to pay are the government taxes. Most contest rules will specifically state that you are responsible for all taxes and any other monies you choose to spend (e.g. spending money on a trip or to upgrade a car). The taxes (e.g. airport and hotel) or the customs and duties (due on a prize won in the United States being shipped to Canada—see *Tax Implications?),* are payable to the Canadian government and do not go to the sponsor or contest management company.

TIP: When you win a trip, it's a cheap trip, not a free trip. An example of this is when you win the airfare and hotel stay, you are responsible for all other monies spent on the trip: meals, taxis, tours, souvenirs, gratuities, etc. Ensure you budget for vacations if you are entering to win trips.

In twenty plus years of infrequent contesting and four years of daily contesting I have only ever had one "winning" phone call asking for my credit card number so I could receive my prize. I told them I knew it was a scam and they promptly hung up. I do get dozens of emails, on a daily basis, informing me I won the lottery in some foreign country. My spam filtering software promptly dumps most of those into my Deleted Folder—that is one way to easily spot a legitimate congratulatory email from a fraudulent one.

A legitimate congratulatory call, letter or email will offer you information that 1) you will probably remember (the contest name) and 2) contact information you can easily verify (e.g. employee, company phone number, address, etc.) If you are unsure, have a friend or relative investigate for you, such as doing an Internet search or contacting the company to verify the contest information.

If you get one of these fraudulent phone calls, emails or letters, get as much information as you can (in the case of a phone call) and forward the information to the authorities.

Let's help end fraud.

The RCMP (Royal Canadian Mounted Police), the OPP (Ontario Provincial Police), the Competition Bureau and the Federal Government have set up **PhoneBusters** (www.phonebusters.com) to stop fraud. This coalition was originally intended to stop telephone scams. Due to the advent of the Internet and the globalization of fraud, they not only try to stop all fraud in Canada but work with the authorities worldwide to stop fraud and catch these con artists globally.

You can report any suspicious activity to PhoneBusters at the same toll free number in the Canada or the United States.

> Toll Free: 1-888-495-8501
> Overseas and Local: 1-705-495-8501
> Toll Free Fax Number: 1-888-654-9426
> Fax Number (Overseas and Local): 1-705-494-4008
> Mailing Address: Box 686, North Bay, Ontario P1B 8J8
> E-mail: info@phonebusters.com

If the con-artists are no longer able to dupe people into giving them money, the scams and fraud will stop.

Tax Implications?

In the United States, taxes are due on any winnings with a value of more than $600 USD. In Canada we do not pay taxes on winnings of any kind. (The exception may be if your employer is holding an internal contest. The prize may be considered a taxable employee benefit. Check with your Human Resources and/or Accounting Department.)

I was told of one contest in particular that wanted the winner's SIN (Social Insurance Number) to release the prize. This was a contest run by a US contest management company and assumed the procedure to release a prize was the same in Canada as it was in the US. If you win a prize from the US, you are not required to pay tax or release your SIN.

What is the Social Insurance Number (SIN)?
The Social Insurance Number (SIN) was created in 1964 to serve as a client account number in the administration of the Canada Pension Plan and Canada's varied employment insurance programs. In 1967, what is now Canada Revenue Agency (CRA) started using the SIN for tax reporting purposes.

Why do organizations ask for it?
Organizations in and outside government ask for the SIN because it is a simple method of identification. Many use it as a client account number to save them from setting up their own numbering systems.

Although only certain government departments and programs are authorized to collect and use the SIN, there is no legislation that prohibits organizations asking for it.

Why is my SIN so important to personal information and privacy?
The SIN may be a key piece of information to open the door to your personal information.

Computer technology makes it possible to use the SIN to find and match your information from one database to another; without your knowledge, a detailed profile could be drawn about you. This amounts to "data surveillance" or monitoring of your daily life, which can pose a serious threat to our privacy and autonomy.

Your SIN can be used to steal your identity. Along with other personal information, someone may be able to use your SIN to apply for a credit card or open a bank account, rent vehicles, equipment, or accommodations in your name, leaving you responsible for the bills, charges, bad checks, and taxes.

Who can ask for my SIN?
Your SIN is a confidential number that is restricted to income reporting purposes. There are a select and limited number of federal government departments and programs specifically authorized to collect the SIN.

The authority to collect and use the SIN is tied to a specific legislated purpose, not necessarily to a particular body. For example, an employer can collect an employee's SIN to provide them with Records of Employment and T-4 slips for income tax purposes, as can provincial or municipal agencies to report financial assistance payments for income tax purposes.

Institutions from which you earn interest or income, such as banks, credit unions and trust companies, must also ask for your SIN.

So, what can I do when asked for my SIN?
Ask if you are required by law to provide it; ask why the person needs it, how it will be used and to whom it will be given.

Your SIN is not a piece of identification. If it is not required by law (and you are not satisfied with the explanation), tell the person you prefer not to use the SIN and offer other identification;

If the organization refuses to give you the product or service unless you give your SIN, complain to the Privacy Commissioner of Canada;

If you would like better legal protection for your SIN, call or write your federal Member of Parliament.

Source: *Fact Sheet: Social Insurance Number (SIN)*, **Privacy Commissioner of Canada 2004. Reproduced with the permission of the Minister of Public Works and Government Services Canada, 2005. www.privcom.gc.ca/fs-fi/02_05_d_02_e.asp**

No one can withhold a product or service if you refuse to give out your SIN.

Remember, giving out your SIN to an unauthorized party ties in to fraud and scams. DO NOT give out any personal information you are uncomfortable with.

Be aware, if you win from a US-based contest, you will probably have to pay customs, duties and taxes on the prize when it crosses the border. If an item has a value of more then $20.00 CAD then taxes generally apply. The total amount you have to pay will be determined by the shipping method. Items shipped via courier will have a higher fee because they have customs brokers that clear all items so they can get across the border in a timely manner. Canada Post charges a small fee (approx. $5.00) to clear a package above the taxes owed to the CRA (Canada Revenue Agency).

You can refuse to accept the package and not pay the customs, duties and taxes. The package will be returned to the sender. As a courtesy you should notify the contest management company or sponsor and let them know why you refused the package.

Some prizes may be detained or even refused at the border. Items such as weapons, fresh fruit/vegetables, meat, chemicals, plants, tobacco, and alcohol may face quarantines or might be refused altogether. You may not want to even enter such contests the prize could be detained or refused at the border.

If you do pay custom charges, you can fill out the form attached to your package (or see link below) and request a reassessment and possible refund. If you enclose a copy of your win notice and a letter stating the item was a win and therefore free, you have a good chance of having the custom charges refunded.

For more information visit the Canada Revenue Agency's web site at: www.cra-arc.gc.ca/tax/business/topics/gst/individual/taxable/ importsexports/importedgoods_indv-e.html

The GST rebate form can be located here: www.cra-arc.gc.ca/tax/business/topics/gst/individual/rebates/general-e.html

Government Regulations
Contesting Problems

If you have a problem with a contest your first course of action is to complain to the contest management company. Most companies are in business to make money. Their objective is to keep their client's customers happy so they will usually do their best to resolve any issues you may have.

The two most common problems you may try to get resolved are problems with the contest itself (e.g. unclear or conflicting rules, problems with the online entry form, etc.) or when trying to obtain a prize (e.g. the prize is extraordinarily late in arriving, not the prize stated you would receive, etc.)

If you are not satisfied with that resolution, speak to the marketing department of the sponsoring company. The sponsor is paying the contest management company to promote their products and services along with attracting new customers. It's in their best interests to have happy winners of their contests telling all their friends how wonderful the product or experience was, so usually they will do what they can to solve any problems that come up.

If you are still unsatisfied, the last course of action would be to complain to the government.

Who regulates contests and games of chance?

All three levels of government—federal, provincial and municipal—have jurisdiction over contests and games of chance.

The federal government, through Industry Canada, provides information and examines complaints regarding contests, draws and sweepstakes in relation to the promotional contest provision of the Competition Act.

Municipalities also license and regulate games of chance; their jurisdiction is determined largely, but not entirely, by the dollar value of the prizes offered.

The provinces regulate and license all of the activities listed for municipalities when the prizes are large, as well as bingos, fairs and exhibitions.

Federal

If you wish to complain about a promotion, you will need to do so through Industry Canada with the exception of Quebec who must go through the Régie des alcools, des courses et des jeux.

Promotional Contests
Section 74.06 of the *Competition Act*, which is a civil provision, prohibits any promotional contest that does not disclose the number and approximate value of prizes, the area or areas to which they relate and any important information relating to the chances of winning such as the odds of winning. It also stipulates that the distribution of prizes cannot be

unduly delayed and that participants be selected or
prizes distributed on the basis of skill or on a random
basis. It should be noted that in addition to complying
with section 74.06 of the Act, a contest must be
lawful as it relates to other federal statutes such as the
Criminal Code, as well as other relevant provincial
statutes and local by-laws. The possible applicability
of these statutes and by-laws should be explored.
If a court determines that a person has engaged in
conduct contrary to section 74.06 it may order the
person not to engage in such conduct, to publish a
corrective notice and/or to pay an administrative
monetary penalty of up to $50,000 in the case of a
first time occurrence by an individual and $100,000
in the case of a first time occurrence by a corporation.
For subsequent orders, the penalties increase to a
maximum of $100,000 in the case of an individual
and $200,000 in the case of a corporation.
www.competitionbureau.gc.ca/Internet/index.cfm?ite
mID=1210&lg=e

Marketing Practices - Prohibitions
The Bureau is responsible for the administration and
enforcement of the *Competition Act*, a law of general
application governing most business conduct in
Canada as well as three laws promoting fair
representation in the marketing of consumer
products: namely the *Consumer Packaging and
Labelling Act*, the *Textile Labelling Act*, and the
Precious Metals Marking Act.

The *Competition Act* contains criminal and civil
provisions to address false or misleading
representations and deceptive marketing practices in
promoting the supply or use of a product or any
business interest.

Under the criminal regime, the general provision
prohibits all materially false or misleading

representations made knowingly or recklessly. Other provisions specifically prohibit deceptive telemarketing, deceptive notices of winning a prize, double ticketing, and schemes of pyramid selling. The multi-level marketing provisions define the responsibilities of operators and participants in multi-level marketing plans.

Under the civil regime, the general provision prohibits all materially false or misleading representations. Other provisions specifically prohibit performance representations not based on adequate and proper tests, misleading warranties and guarantees, false or misleading ordinary selling price representations, untrue, misleading or unauthorized use of tests and testimonials, bait and switch selling, and the sale of a product above its advertised price. The promotional contest provisions set out the requirements for conducting a contest, lottery, or game of chance or skill. www.competitionbureau.gc.ca/Internet/index.cfm?ite mID=1171&lg=e

Deceptive Notices of Winning a Prize
Section 53 of the *Competition Act*, which is a criminal provision, prohibits the sending of a notice that gives the recipient the general impression he or she has won a "prize" or other benefit and asks or gives the option to pay money or incur a cost in order to obtain the prize or benefit. The provision applies to notices sent by any means, including but not limited to regular or electronic mail. No offence would arise if the recipient actually receives the prize or benefit and the person who sent the notice: (1) provides fair and adequate disclosure of the number and approximate value of prizes or benefits, the area or areas to which they have been allocated, and any fact that materially affects the chances of winning; (2) distributes prizes without unreasonable delay; and (3)

139

selects participants or distributes prizes randomly or on the basis of participants' skill, in any area to which the prizes or benefits have been allocated.

Any person who contravenes section 53 is guilty of an offence and liable to a fine of up to $200,000 and/or imprisonment up to one year on summary conviction, or to fines in the discretion of the court and/or imprisonment up to five years upon indictment.
www.competitionbureau.gc.ca/Internet/index.cfm?ite mID=1206&lg=e

How to File a Complaint
You may request information or submit a complaint against an organization that adopts business practices which may be in violation with the *Competition Act*, the *Consumer Packaging and Labelling Act*, the *Textile Labelling Act* and the *Precious Metals Marking Act* administered by the Competition Bureau.

If you wish to file a complaint regarding a deceptive business practice, here is what we need to know to help you:
> **Personal Information**: Tell us about yourself. Please note that the information collected in this section is protected under the *Privacy Act*.
> **Target of Complaint**: Tell us about the company or organization that you have a complaint against.
> **Details of Complaint**: Tell us about your complaint. Provide us with detailed information using products and or services supplied, products name and description.

We suggest you use the On-Line Complaint/Enquiry Form to file a complaint but you can contact the

Information Centre through e-mail for additional information or comments at: compbureau@cb-bc.gc.ca.

You might prefer to contact the Information Centre by phone or by facsimile.
    Monday - Friday, 8:30 to 5 p.m., EST.
    Toll-free: 1 800 348-5358
    TDD (for hearing impaired): 1 800 642-3844
    Fax: (819) 997-0324

If you chose to mail your complaint, the address is:
    Competition Bureau
    50 Victoria Street
    Gatineau, Quebec
    K1A 0C9

www.competitionbureau.gc.ca/Internet/index.cfm?ite mID=130&lg=e

Online Enquiry/Complaint Form:
https://www.competitionbureau.gc.ca/Internet/index.cfm?itemID=1260&lg=e&CFID=284281&CFTOKEN=62235492

Reproduced with the permission of The Minister of Public Works and Government Services, 2005

Provincial

You would want to contact the provincial and municipal governments to obtain permits and licenses if you are interested in holding any type of gaming activity. Many organizations do this (e.g. soccer and hockey clubs, school and church groups, etc.) when they want to raise money for their group or club by holding a raffle, casino night or bingo. Check with your province's regulations as some of these activities are licensed through your local municipality.

YOU CAN'T WIN IF YOU DON'T ENTER

ALBERTA
Department of Gaming
www.gaming.gov.ab.ca

BRITISH COLUMBIA
Gaming Policy and Enforcement Branch
www.pssg.gov.bc.ca/gaming

NEW BRUNSWICK
Department of Public Safety
http://app.infoaa.7700.gnb.ca/gnb/pub/DetailOrgEng1.asp?OrgID1=43
23&DeptID1=78
www.gnb.ca/0276/publications/lottlic_e.pdf

NEWFOUNDLAND
Department of Government Services, Lotteries
www.gs.gov.nl.ca/cca/tpl/lotteries.stm

NORTHWEST TERRITORY
Municipal and Community Affairs
www.maca.gov.nt.ca/about/corporate_affairs.html
www.maca.gov.nt.ca/resources/forms.html#lottery

NOVA SCOTIA
Alcohol and Gaming Authority
www.gov.ns.ca/aga/defaultindex.htm
www.gov.ns.ca/snsmr/paal/ndxgame.asp

NUNAVAT
NOTE: No website is available for Nunavut at this time.

MANITOBA
Manitoba Gaming Control Commission
www.mgcc.mb.ca/faq/gaming_in_mb.html

ONTARIO
Alcohol and Gaming Commission of Ontario
www.agco.on.ca

QUEBEC
Régie des alcools des courses et des jeux
www.racj.gouv.qc.ca

PRINCE EDWARD ISLAND
Office of the Attorney General
www.gov.pe.ca/infopei/index.php3?number=14973&lang=E

SASKATCHEWAN
Saskatchewan Liquor and Gaming Authority
www.slga.gov.sk.ca

YUKON
Lotteries Yukon
www.ylc.yk.ca/lotteries.html

Municipal

Check with your local municipal government. It would be impractical
for me to list every agency and department for every municipality in
Canada responsible for lotteries and gaming.

*"The best luck of all is the luck you
make for yourself."*
Douglas Macarthur

CONTEST DEVELOPMENT AND MANAGEMENT COMPANIES

One thing I have noticed over the past few years is contestors have many questions regarding contests and their rules. They are debated in newsletters and online groups, yet no one has contacted these companies to find out what the true answers are. I had the pleasure of interviewing some of the biggest contest management companies and judging agencies in Canada. I interviewed each company separately and to avoid repetition, I consolidated their answers into a virtual roundtable discussion.

IC Group Inc. (IC)

IC Group Inc. (www.icgroupinc.com) was formed in 1989 and has offices in Canada, the United States and the UK. IC Group specializes in designing and delivering secure promotions including collect and scratch to win, sweepstakes, and online games/contests. They offer a service called Promotion Risk Management to assist contest sponsors in preventing contest errors or security breaches. They also offer insurance for promotional programs covering liability for prize pools and events such as hole-in-ones and event cancellation/non-appearance.

Duncan McCready, Executive Vice President in their Toronto office, was kind enough to answer all my questions.

Launchfire Interactive (LF)

Launchfire Interactive (www.launchfire.com) located in Ottawa, ON, was started in 1999 by John Findley and A.J. Pratt as an interactive advertising company. They began to tie contests into their promotions so their clients could learn more about their customers and develop one-to-one communications with the consumer.

It was an interesting interview because I was only able to ask John about half the questions. Many of the Internet questions did not apply because the interactive marketing system they have created eliminated many of the problems encountered by contestors. None of the mail-in questions applied because their company only handles Internet based contests.

NOTE: Many contests have a mail-in NPE (No Purchase Entry) option. Since Launchfire's contests are no-purchase, they are not required to have a mail-in option.

Launchfire offers an online subscription called GameWatch to announce when new games and contests are released. To get your free subscription, go to www.launchfire.com.

Marco Sales and Incentives Limited (MS)

I had a wonderful interview with Scott Cruickshank of Marco Sales and Incentives Limited (www.marcosales.com). They began in 1973 as a promotional fulfillment company and have grown to offer many other services including contest and sweepstake management. Marco Sales recently moved to a new facility in Brantford, ON. They have, however made special arrangements with Canada Post to keep their very famous Paris, ON, contest entry mailing address.

N5R (N5R)

I met with Roman Bodnarchuk, CEO at N5R (www.n5r.com) at his office in downtown Toronto, ON. They develop online contest for both Canadian and US clients as part of a complete promotional program. Roman feels the odds of contesting on the Internet currently is very good and will decrease over time as more people adapt to the technology.

Promodem Media Inc. (PM)

I meet with Steve Bush, owner of Promodem Media Inc. (www.promodem.com). Located in Uxbridge, ON they specialize in contest and sweepstake hosting services along with advergame development.

They operate and manage the website www.canadiannetstakes.com which hosts the contests they are promoting, games and a community forum area.

Publicis Dialog (PD)

Publicis Groupe began in 1926 and includes three independently operated worldwide networks: Leo Burnett Worldwide, Publicis Worldwide and Saatchi & Saatchi Worldwide, as well as two multi-hub creative networks: BBH and Fallon.

I spoke with Corrine Katz, an Account Director with Public Dialog (www.publicis.ca) a division of Publicis Worldwide.

Resolve Corporation (RC)

Resolve Corporation (www.resolvecorporation.com) united all their former companies (BDP, DDS, NCH Watts and Watts Communications) under one integrated brand as of May 2004. Due to company's size and the extensive number of services they offer, I did not get to the opportunity to interview them in person. Wayne Mouland, Director of Analytical Services was kind enough to assist me in getting the questions answered.

SplashDot (SD)

SplashDot (www.splashdot.com) was started in 1998 by Patrick Watson and Jonathan Csakany. Their specialty is promotions and loyalty programs designed to be fun, entertaining and to get the participant to play an active role in the contest.

They also manage the SuperPages.ca Contest Directory (http://contests.superpages.ca/cd/contest.asp). It's a listing of the contests they manage or additional contests their clients are running.

When answering a skill testing question (STQ) is the question to be answered left to right (in order given) or using BEDMAS? e.g. 4+8x2= 24 (L-R) or 20 (BEDMAS)

This is the number one question asked of me and within the contesting groups I belong to, because if the STQ is answered improperly a win could turn into a loss.

MS stated that, "A good question should be written properly so that the answer would be the same using either left to right order of operations or BEDMAS. We want our contests to be easy for people to enter and not lose because a skill testing question (STQ) was confusing or complicated. Smaller companies running their own contests may not understand this and that's why you see poorly laid out STQs."

The best way to lay out a STQ to avoid any confusion is to write the STQ out so it covers several lines, uses full words. For example:

   Multiply 38 by 5
   Divide by 2
   Add 122
   Minus 57
   Answer = 160

LF said, "Our questions are presented to the potential winner over the phone and are very straight forward. Our representative reads them the question in the order that it is to be calculated. They do follow the BEDMAS format if anyone was to study the order. All of our potential winners get the skill testing questions correct since the format we present them in is so simple."

Only **IC** said, "Our skill testing questions are verified here based on left-to-right."

TIP: If you have any doubt as to how the question should be answered, ASK!

By Canadian contesting regulations we must answer a skill testing question in order to win. Is there a standard by which questions are designed or is it up to the contest developer?

All the companies had the same answer. **N5R** said, "There is no standard at the moment. It is up to the developer or their client to design the question."

Is there a rule or regulation that a contestant must put down their correct age?
Are there any hard and fast rules to the age a contestant can be?

Many people do not like to put down their correct age because they do not want to appear "old". The reason age is asked is to determine if the contestant can legally win the contest. **PM** said, "The rules should be read to determine if you are eligible to enter a contest. So if it states the contestant must be the age of majority and the entrant is only seventeen, then they are ineligible and would be disqualified if their name was drawn. If they are under age and allowed to enter the contest, then a parent or guardian would need to sign the release forms if their name was drawn."

To avoid this problem, **LF**'s system, "does not ask for your specific age but what age bracket you fall into. For example 18-34, 34-49 etc."

There is a rule regarding age as **IC** stated, "Yes—In both Canada and the US, contestants must have parental consent if they are under the age of 13."

If a family shares the same e-mail address (thesmiths@anywhere.com) and the contest is one entry per person, how do you scan the files for duplicates because if both John and Jane Smith entered the only field that would differ is the first name?

Most of the contest administrators search for duplicate entries electronically. **IC** told me "Duplicate searches are conducted electronically. The guidelines for duplicate entries would be determined by contest sponsor. Best efforts are made to limit one entry per email address." **MS** added that "Most contests that state one entry per person also state one entry per email address. In this case only one person could enter because they share an email address." **PD** said, "It depends on the rules. We can scan for either on the name field or the e-mail field. If the e-mail field is scanned we would disqualify the second entry," and **SD** said, "The e-mail field is a unique field so they may not be able to enter twice in situations where this is set out as a requirement. This should be identified in the rules."

However, not all the companies would discard duplicates out of hand. **N5R** said, "Sometimes yes and sometimes no. It depends on the contest so we recommend everyone reads the rules and regulations." So, once again, remember my number one tip: *read the rules of the contest.*

TIP: Each person entering online contests in a household should have their own e-mail address.

What happens if someone enters both a husband and a wife then realizes that the contest is one entry per household? Do you disqualify both entries or just remove the extra one?

This is a tricky one because as **MS** stated, "Maybe yes and maybe no. Some contests entries are not sorted so both entries would be in the contest. Some contests are sorted and the duplicate is kicked out so the one entry has an equal chance in the contest. Some contests are very specific about duplicate entries and if sorted both would be deleted." **SD** said, "We always scan for duplicates and we would typically disqualify both entries, depending upon the official rules of the contest in question."

On the other hand, **PM** feels most people are entering contests because they want to win. They are not out to cheat the contest management company or the sponsor. "When we do a search after the draw to determine if the potential winner cheated and see two similar entries entered at different times during the contest period and it appears to be an honest error, we would alert our client and let them make the determination if the want to award the prize to that person or redraw for the prize." **PD** said, "We always keep the first entry and disqualify all subsequent entries."

TIP: If you wish to keep track of the contests you enter, use either a manual log or use a program such as Turbo Sweeps.

If someone says no to having a company contact them via email or any other means, are they also denying them permission to be contacted if they win?

Companies ask this question because they want permission to market their products and services to you in the future. All the companies had the same answer. **PM** said, "No. The permission is for opt-in lists so the contestant can receive information at a later date. It does not affect the contest entry."

NOTE: Remember, there are two schools of thought on this subject and you should decide for yourself you choose to follow. The first is: to cut down on spam, always opt-out. The second is: if you wish to be notified of contests and promotions from sites and companies that run them on a regular basis, opt-in.

RC had a very good explanation of opt-in vs. opt-out and the validity of your entry. "Giving permission for a marketer to verify eligibility to win a prize and giving permission for follow-up contact for other reasons are two separate issues.

"By entering, a contest entrant agrees to abide by the contest rules, which includes allowing the contest manager to contact them if their entry is selected as a potential winner. In fact, contest rules usually state that the contest manager will contact each potential winner to administer a test of skill and to verify that they qualify as a winner.

"Permission for follow-up contact by the marketer is a separate issue and may be applied as an opt-in clause on the contest entry form."

In the rules you often see "one per household" or "one per person" or "one per email address"—why are they not more specific such as one per household?

This is the second most frequently asked question. It is because the rules are generally written to satisfy the lawyers and not the contestant: as stated by **PM**, "It is worded that particular way for legal reasons." **SD** had the easiest way to determine what the entry parameters were. "If the rules seem unclear, always go with the overlaying restriction, which in this case is one entry per household." **MS** added, "The rules should really state either one per household, or one per person or email address, not all three. We have a specialist here that writes over 450 sets of rules (on average) for contests in a given year. We pride ourselves on having clear rules that are legally correct, comply with Canada's regulations and are easy for a contestor to understand."

If the rules do not state the number of entries such as one-time only, daily, weekly or monthly, how many entries should a contestor assume?

My response to all contestors that ask me that question is to ask the company running the contest. **SD** said, "About two-thirds of all contests have poor quality issues. Not stating the number of entries is one of them. We always state the number of entries allowed."

You will find that all contests run by a professional contest management companies will always have the limitation stated in the rules. If a company chooses to run a promotion without hiring a management company, call or write them asking for clarification and requesting the rules be more specific in all aspects including number of entries.

If the contest rules state one entry per electronic address, how does more than one person per household enter a one entry per person contest?

N5R said, "One per electronic address means one per email address." An IP or electronic address is different than an email address. An IP address is the address of your computer.

As stated before, **IC** "That a person would have to have a separate email account set up in order to get around the one email address per household requirement."

TIP: There are a number of free e-mail services, such as Hotmail and Yahoo Mail. If anyone in your household needs a unique email address to enter contests with, this is a simple way to go about it without having to spend any money.

When a contest is daily or has multiple entries, do you ever just group the entries together at the end and eliminate the duplicates? Is it really worthwhile to enter every day?

All of the companies had the same basic answer: enter as often as you are allowed. **PM** said "Yes [it is worthwhile to enter] because it increases your total number of entries in the draw." **SD** agreed, "YES!! Enter as often as the rules state you can." **MS** added, "We do not lump entries together. If a contest can be entered daily over a one month period and you enter every day you have thirty entries, if you enter every other day you have fifteen entries. The more you enter the more chances you have to win."

So remember, enter early and as often as you are allowed by the rules. You have nothing to lose by entering often.

What is the definition of weekly? Someone may enter on a Friday (week one) and then try to enter again on Monday (week two) getting the message "you have already entered this week." Is a week Sunday-Saturday or week to week based to the date and time of the first entry?

SD said, "Read the rules because it depends on the promotion and the start date of the contests. We fully outline the weekly dates in our rules so a participant will be very clear on when they can enter." **RC** added, "How a week is defined may vary by contest. For the Internet contests, unless otherwise stated in the rules, Resolve would take this to mean that a contestant can only enter once per 7-day period. For mail-in contests, this restriction would be one entry per calendar week (received mail)." For **PM** it is a bit different. "Many of our clients are in the media industry so we base weekly on the broadcast week which is Monday to Sunday."

Do you really check every e-mail to make sure someone didn't accidentally enter twice in a one entry contest?

PD stated, "Yes. We always scan for duplicate entries." **MS** said, "We do not host every contest on our web servers since many companies want to drive consumer traffic to their website and we just receive a file at the end of the contest period. The company may or may not have "cleansed" the file before sending it to us. We do a sort or a cleanse if requested by our client."

If someone forgets they entered a contest, if a warning comes up saying "you have already entered," have they disqualified themselves?
If a warning does not come up, what do you do with the accidental duplicates?

PM said, "No, they have not disqualified themselves. The polite message is called a Repeat Entry Block. It allows us to block cheaters and prevents the honest contestant from accidentally disqualifying themselves. I am not sure why more companies do not use that feature when designing a promotion." **PD** agrees, "We always give a polite warning message so someone doesn't accidentally disqualify themselves. If for some reason the warning did not come up we would eliminate the duplicate entries. The reason all promotions do not have a warning in place is the added cost."

Sometimes a website is functional before the actual start date. Do you erase all entries before that date and someone can come back and re-enter if they did so previously by error, or do you keep all entries regardless of entry date?

A promotion should not be made "live" before the official start date as outlined in the rules. **MS** explained why this may occur. "Sometimes an online contest entry page is active before the start date for testing purposes. We delete all entries received before the start date. If someone accidentally entered a one entry only contest before the start date, they could come back and re-enter."

Everyone else had the same position. **SD** said, "Not our contests. If, for some reason, someone did enter before the start date and time, we would do what is known as a data dump to clear the database. Again the rules take priority here—so if they state the contest starts on a certain date, then all entries from that date are included. It would be wrong to include anything previous to the start date or anything after the end date."

If a contest offers a tell-a-friend space on the contest page, is telling the friend mandatory to receiving an entry into the contest?

This question got several different points of view. **SD** said, "This is called *viral marketing*. It will depend on the client and what is appropriate for the promotion whether or not we give additional entries for referrals. If additional entries are provided, this is a great way of maximizing entries—but friends should be real people since there is always a possibility of disqualification if the friend who you signed up turns out to be a false name." **LF** added, "We offer a bonus entry for referring friends so we encourage referral by rewarding the player with extra entries." **N5R** felt the same way. "We encourage referrals by offering bonus entries but they are not mandatory for the initial entry."

PM had an interesting point. "On some promotions we have an incentive to tell-a-friend and some we don't. 30% of the entrants will refer a friend even without the incentive to do so."

NOTE: There are two types of referral bonus entries: direct and closed-loop. The direct referral will give you a bonus entry into the contest, just for referring someone. The closed-loop will only give you a bonus entry if the person you referred returns to the website and enters the promotion themselves. This is usually tracked by an email sent to the referral with a unique URL back to the promotion website.

Are your chances of winning better with online or mail-in? This one leads to a question on the industry in general—Do you think mail-in contests will disappear in time with Internet contesting becoming the standard?

This question is a matter of new technology vs. "old school." Everyone had the same answer regarding the odds as stated by **IC**. "The chances of winning are the same for online and mail-in."

There were mixed feelings regarding the disappearance of mail-in promotions and the timeline that would occur in. **IC** felt, "To state that mail-in contests will disappear would be an over-statement. There are still many benefits of marketing and promoting in the offline world. That said, we are conducting more and more online contests. As

Internet usage continues to increase across the world, marketing over the Internet is also."

MS stated, "If a contest has both a mail-in and an online entry option, the letters are numbered as they arrive. At the end of the contest, a random number is generated from a computer and that number is matched to the winning entry regardless if it came in electronically or via the post office. The trend is definitely moving away from mail-in contests to online contesting. I think mail-in contesting may disappear as early as five years from now. In-store ballot entries, however, will remain strong because retailers want to drive foot traffic into their stores." **PD** added, "I do not think mail-in contest will disappear 100%. Not in the near future anyway. I have noticed the call-in entry option has virtually disappeared. The online entry form has replaced that entry option." **SD** said, "There is rarely any purely mail-in contests any more. Mail-in contests are very expensive to run so most of our clients are leaning toward online promotions. I do not think mail-in contests will disappear entirely as our clients do not want to alienate anyone. Many online promotions now have a mail-in component."

When the rules state one entry and it's a mail-in or ballot box, how is that enforced?

In the past there may not have been away to enforce this rule with thousands of entries coming in to any given contest. Technology, however, has changed the playing field. It doesn't pay to cheat. (see *Good Karma*.)

IC said, "It depends on the contest mechanic, and how contest entries are handled. Typically, received entries are entered into a database and then a random electronic drawing is conducted to determine an eligible winner. In this situation, duplicate entries would be filtered out electronically within the data management process." **PM added.** "We check all entries at the end of every contest to determine if anyone has cheated. It is very easy with the online entries to so a search for cheaters."

If someone is lucky enough to keep winning various contests, do you discard their name so other people can win, or do you actually

let those people win over and over again if they are that lucky to have their name picked?
Who oversees the drawing to ensure you are following Canadian contesting regulations?

If you always follow the rules and are very lucky, you can win, over and over.

MS said, "We recognize names from various contests and do not bar people from winning. There is an elderly gentleman living in Paris, Ontario, and his hobby is contesting. He wins several contests per year and the local paper usually does an annual story on him. We also had one woman win the same contest two years in a row. The odds against that are phenomenal." **N5R** agreed, "We would let their name be re-picked since each promotion is separate. If they are lucky enough to have their name selected a few times then they are very, very lucky."

Each company has its own drawing procedures but each is handled in a very professional manner. **IC** said, "In contests where we are appointed as the third party judging organization to oversee and conduct a drawing, we develop the draw process and arrange for the appropriate parties to be present at the draw. Such parties may include representatives of the Contest Sponsor and/or other third party representatives. Videotaping of draw procedures and administration of draw affidavits is completed to properly document the required draw procedures. Some draws may require the involvement of third party adjudicators and we would be responsible for the appointment of such adjudicators in such instances. Third party adjudicators are typically licensed claims adjusters." **MS** added, "We have a standard procedure that we follow and two officials oversee the draw and take minutes. We work closely with lawyer Brenda Pritchard who specializes in contest law at Gowling Lafleur Henderson." **SD** stated, "It would depend on the client who would oversee the drawing. Most have their own security people attend and the draws are video taped."

How do they actually select a winner from the online entries?
Is it done with a computer program or does an official randomly pick a number?

Is each entry given a number and the winning number is predetermined?

All the companies had similar answers. **N5R** said, "We use a software package designed to select random numbers. We then match that number given to a contest entry. Most companies use their own internal legal department to ensure they are following regulations." **SD** added, "The winner is selected via a software program that chooses random persons from the pool of entrants. It is worth noting that we have Active Cheat Deterrence—if a person has entered more than once, even with slightly different information, our system will likely identify them as a potential cheater."

If it is a one time only entry, is there a better chance of winning if you enter early or late in the contest?

It makes no difference to your odds of winning if it is one entry only contests. Enter anytime during the contest entry period. However, if you can enter the contests daily then do so. **LF** said, "There is no difference if you enter early or late in our contests. However, since we give each player an extra entry for coming back each day they will have more ballots in the draw the earlier they start." **N5R** added, "Enter early since many promotions draw weekly." And **SD** stated, "It's like the lottery balls. Some go into the machine first yet the numbers that come out are totally random. Everything needs to be random in order to be fair to all entrants."

Married or common law, is it the same thing when it comes to contesting?

All the companies had the same answer. **RC** said, "The marital status of any contestant would not matter unless the rules stated that it did." One entry per household is one entry per household.

If the mother's last name is different than the children's, should she enter the father in as the guardian or can she put her name?

Again, everyone had a similar response to this question. **LF** said, "There are stringent laws regarding children and contesting. As long as the parent or legal guardian gives their permission, it does not matter if the last names are different. This is also becoming more and more common for the mother to retain her maiden name and have it be different than the child's." **MS** added, "It is very common now for mothers to have a different last name than her children. As long as she is a legal guardian (parent) of the child(ren) then she can use her name when giving permission for the child's contest entry."

Many contests have an "optional" questionnaire attached to them. What if someone doesn't fill it in? Will their entry be disregarded even though the questions are not compulsory?
If a contest with a questionnaire is a daily entry, do you expect people to fill out the questionnaire each time or is the first time sufficient?

PM succinctly said, "Optional means optional. No, they would not be disqualified. We also feel there should be a registration page and a login page for contests. That would eliminate the requirement to fill out the questionnaire for every entry." (see *Opt-In or Opt-Out?*) **SD** repeated my number one tip, "Always read the rules to see if the questionnaire is compulsory or optional in the entry process and enter accordingly." **PD** agreed, "If it is optional it does not have to be filled in the first time or on subsequent entries. However if the questionnaire is mandatory for the entry then yes, it must be filled in each and every time. Read the rules to determine the entry qualifications if it not clear on the entry form."

What happens to unclaimed prizes?

This was one of the most interesting questions put forth because each company had a slightly different answer.

IC said, "The rules would disclose this information. If the rules state 'all unclaimed prizes will be awarded via a random draw at the end of the contest,' then that is what will happen. Otherwise, unclaimed prizes are not awarded and the Contest Sponsor need not disclose anything further."

LF said, "We draw ten names for each contest. We start with the first name drawn. If the prize is unclaimed we go to the second name, etc...We have never had a prize go unclaimed, although we have had to contact more than one person on the list before a prize was claimed."

MS said, "If the contest is a sweepstakes, then alternate names are drawn for people that do not claim their prize after notification. If the contest is an instant win, the companies sponsoring the contest do not pre-purchase 100% of the prizes since not 100% are claimed. Many winning cards, cups, boxes, etc. are either not noticed or thrown away."

(I can hear many die hard contestors gasping at the thought of a large win being thrown out!)

N5R said, "We return them to our clients. Now, we do go through several methods to contact the winners before we give up on that contestant. We send an e-mail, phone, fax—if applicable, mail them a letter, and at that point if they do not respond we either move to the next name or return the prizes, again depending on the contest rules."

PM said, "We keep selecting entrants until all the prizes have been awarded."

PD said, "We keep drawing names until the prize is claimed."

SD said, "It depends on the promotion. We generally redraw if the contestant does not claim the prize. However, we have had instant win contests where only a portion of the prizes were claimed. We do not give out the balance."

RC said, "If it is not spelled out in the rules, the sponsor determines what happens to any unclaimed prizes."

NOTE: If you are entering contests, respond to any e-mails, phone calls or letters you may receive congratulating you on your potential win. They are not a scam. I have won many prizes and discovered while talking with the contest management company my ballot was not the first one drawn. I was, however, the first one to respond. (See Scams to determine the difference between a real notification and a fraudulent one.)

What happens if someone doesn't receive their prize?
How do you ensure all prizes are delivered?

Most companies ship with a carrier that requires a signature so the prizes can be traced if necessary. **LF** said, "We use regular mail for small prizes and courier companies for larger prizes. We have never had anyone contact us to say they have not received their prize." **RC** added, "To deliver high value prizes Resolve uses a delivery-company that requires the recipient to sign for the prize, e.g. courier or registered mail. Even with regular mail there are rarely any problems with prize delivery, because we use software that checks the validity of consumer addresses." **MS** stated, "If someone does not receive their win in a timely manner, I suggest they contact the contest management company immediately."

IC said, "It would depend on how the prize was shipped. In some cases we use a delivery method that requires a signature, so we can trace what happened to the prize. If this isn't the case, the contest sponsor would determine a procedure on how to handle a shipment/prize that wasn't received. As above—signature on delivery is preferred."

What do you do with unreadable entries? Do you try to decipher them, or just toss them?
What if an entry says please print your name and address and a person is unable to write due to a disability or a disease?

MS said, "We do everything we can to ensure the winning ballot gets the prize. We have had ballots in the past where only the phone number is legible so we call the winner. If nothing can be read at all we are forced to toss the ballot. If someone can not write legibly, they can use stamps or stickers (such as return address labels). We would prefer that, since we want our contestants to win and not be disqualified due to poor handwriting." **RC** added, "Our experienced processors can usually decipher writing that for many people would be unreadable. Our processors also use software that verifies addresses based on the street address and city name. Nevertheless, it is the responsibility of each contestant to ensure that his or her name and address is correct and legible."

Thankfully, online promotions have removed this problem, as **PM** stated. "Since most entries are online we generally do not have a problem. In the event of a mail-in entry being selected we usually can get enough information off the ballot to contact the winner."

How realistic or "nice" does a hand drawn UPC facsimile have to look?
Many rules say do not use a mechanical device to draw a UPC. Is a ruler considered a mechanical device?
Are both the thick and thin lines required on a hand drawn UPC?

All of the companies had similar answers to this one. **SD** said, "It needs to be reasonable. Most people freehand the UPC and all 12 of the numbers need to be correct along with both thick and thin lines. A ruler is not considered a mechanical device. Most of our contests are moving away from UPCs and going towards essays. It really gets a participant to think about the client and their products or services." **RC** added, "For contests that we manage, if the rules allow a contestant to enter with a hand-drawn facsimile, we would disqualify any entry with a photocopied or scanned proof-of purchase. We would not consider the use of a ruler in drawing a facsimile of a UPC as the use of a mechanical device. The facsimile, however, must also contain all the specific numbers on a valid UPC for the sponsoring product."

Do UPCs sent in with contest entries get checked?

Again, all companies had the same answer as **IC** stated. "Yes -- UPCs are checked."

TIP: Don't have an original Universal Product Code (UPC) handy? Check online. (see Universal Product Codes & Hand Drawn Facsimiles.)

Do decorated, coloured, or odd sized envelopes get drawn more often than a standard #10 envelopes?

MS said, "No. A coloured or decorated envelope does not have a better chance of winning than a plain #10 envelope. All the envelopes are put into a drum and the required number are drawn out. Some people use very large envelopes that do not fit in the drum. We have to put their name on a piece of paper and submit it in the contest. That is why many contests specify a standard size such as a 3x5 card or postcard. This keeps the contest fair and ensures all entries fit in the drum."

For other companies, envelopes don't really matter because there is no drawing drum. Everything is done electronically. **PD** said, "It doesn't matter since we open the envelopes and enter the information into the database." **SD** added, "It's pretty rare that an envelope is drawn anymore. We open the envelopes and enter the contestant's data into a computer."

NOTE: Several of the companies open your envelope and manually enter your data into the computerized sweepstake database. This is important because you are wasting your time by mailing entries into a promotion that possibly has an Internet entry option and/or decorating and embellishing your envelopes.

How much mail do you get in a single day?

IC said, "Mail volume will vary on a daily basis—it can range from hundreds to hundreds of thousands to millions. It depends on the types and number of contests we run at any given time." **MS** added, "Everyday is different. We did have one contest where we got over three million mail-in entries. That had been our largest to date. Some get as few as 5,000 and some get 50,000. Our overall mail delivery is dropping due to the popularity of online contesting."

Other companies indicated a drop in mail due to the advent of online promotions. **PM** said, "We get bins of mail. Most of our contests are run online." And **PD** added, "Not as much as we used to. The volume also depends on how a contest was advertised."

Can a win be altered? Such as, if you win a trip for four to Walt Disney World and you have three children can you buy a fifth ticket?

The answers were varied but it boiled do to, *ask*. You never know until you ask.

LF said, "They may alter the prize based on a personal situation. It is up to the discretion of the contest management company and the sponsor. You have nothing to lose by asking."

MS has a unique situation as, "We have an in-house travel agency to deal with the large volume of trips we give away sponsored by our clients. A prize can possibly be altered. If a trip is for four to Florida and the winner has three children a fifth ticket may be purchased. Or if a trip was for three days, two nights to L.A. an extension may be possible. It would depend on the contest and if the prize was a contra deal. I suggest a winner always ask and they may be able to customize a win."

NOTE: CONTRA is the short form of contract. A contract is a formal agreement between people or groups. A contra agreement is a business-to-business barter arrangement; trading products and/or services for products and/or services. (e.g. trading a hotel stay for magazine advertising.)

Several companies do not do prize administration. **RC** said, "The Resolve Corporation is not a travel agent or promotion agency and does not purchase prizes for its clients. As a result, Resolve would get involved in acting as a mediator between a winner and the marketer to change a prize." **PM** added, "We do not administer the prize after the release form is signed. It would have to be discussed with the contest sponsor."

SD said, "The prize to us is as important as if the winner purchased the product. We would work with the winner and the company to ensure the winner was satisfied with their prize. Sometimes this may mean offering additional prizes at a discount in order to meet the needs of the winner."

NOTE: Remember, the cost of all alterations and additions is the winner's responsibility, so only ask if you can afford the change/alterations.

"When it comes to luck, you make your own."
Bruce Springsteen

ATTRACTING LUCK

There are seven traits and actions I believe winners possess and do.
They are:
1. Think positively.
2. Expect to win.
3. Feel like a winner.
4. Have good *chi* flowing inside and out.
5. Share with others.
6. Don't cheat.
7. Enter, Enter, Enter…

*"Whether you think you can, or
you think you can't, you're right."*
Henry Ford

Positive Thinking

What is your internal dialogue? Is it positive or negative? Are you
always saying, **I can't** or, **I can**? Did you know you *choose* how you
talk to yourself? I have met contestors that say "I never win" or "I am
not lucky" and I think "WOW! If you think that way, you definitely
won't win."

Change your internal and external dialogue. Use *I am*, *I can* and *I will*.
Speak in the present tense as if it has already happened: "I am lucky."
"I am a winner." "I enter as often as I can." "I win often." Pretty soon
you will find those statements and beliefs coming true. Not only when
you contest, in all aspects of your life.

WHO DECIDES WHETHER you shall be happy or
unhappy? The answer—you do!

165

A television celebrity had as a guest on his program an aged man. And he was a very rare old man indeed. His remarks were entirely unpremeditated and of course absolutely unrehearsed. They simply bubbled up out of a personality that was radiant and happy. And whenever he said anything, it was so naive, so apt, that the audience roared with laughter. They loved him. The celebrity was impressed, and enjoyed it with the others.

Finally he asked the old man why he was so happy. "You must have a wonderful secret of happiness," he suggested.

"No," replied the old man, "I haven't any great secret. It's just as plain as the nose on your face. When I get up in the morning," he explained, "I have two choices—either to be happy or to be unhappy, and what do you think I do? I just choose to be happy, and that's all there is to it."

That may seem an oversimplification, and it may appear that the old man was superficial, but I recall that Abraham Lincoln, whom nobody could accuse of being superficial, said that people were just about as happy as they made up their minds to be. You can be unhappy if you want to be. It is the easiest thing in the world to accomplish. Just choose unhappiness. Go around telling yourself that things aren't going well, that nothing is satisfactory, and you can be quite sure of being unhappy. But say to yourself, "Things are going nicely. Life is good. I choose happiness," and you *can* be quite certain of having your choice.

The happiness habit is developed by simply practicing happy thinking. Make a mental list of happy thoughts and pass them through your mind several times every day. If an unhappiness thought should enter your mind, immediately stop, consciously eject it, and substitute a happiness thought. Every morning before arising, lie relaxed in bed and deliberately drop happy thoughts into your conscious mind. Let a series of pictures pass across your mind of each happy experience you expect to have during the day. Savor their joy. Such thoughts will help cause events to turn out that way. Do not affirm that things will not go well that day. By merely saying that, you can actually help to make it so. You will draw to yourself every factor, large and small, that will contribute to unhappy conditions. As a result, you will find yourself asking, "Why does everything go badly for me? What is the matter with everything?"

The reason can be directly traced to the manner in which you begin the day in your thoughts.

Tomorrow try this plan instead. When you arise, say out loud three times this one sentence, "This is the day which the Lord hath made; we will rejoice and be glad in it." (Psalm 118:24) Only personalize it and say, "I will rejoice and be glad in it." Repeat it in a strong, clear voice and with positive tone and emphasis. The statement, of course, is from the Bible and it is a good cure for unhappiness. If you repeat that one sentence three times before breakfast and meditate on the meaning of the words you will change the character of the day by starting off with a happiness psychology.

While dressing or shaving or getting breakfast, say aloud a few such remarks as the following, "I believe this is going to be a wonderful day. I believe I can successfully handle all problems that will arise today. I feel good physically, mentally, emotionally. It is wonderful to be alive. I am grateful for all that I have had, for all that I now have, and for all that I shall have. Things aren't going to fall apart. God is here

and He is with me and He will see me through. I
thank God for every good thing."

*"Luck affects everything; let your hook always be cast.
In the stream where you least expect it, there will be fish."*
Ovid

Expectations

Do you expect to win? I do. If I go to bed at night and I have not won
anything that day I am genuinely disappointed. I am the only person I
know that looks forward to Mondays because the contest management
companies only notify winners during the work week and I can hardly
wait for the next winning call, letter or email.

*NOTE: We have only been notified by a contest management company
of a win on a Saturday once. We have also won online instant win
contests on weekends.*

One of Richard Wiseman's four scientific principles of luck is: Expect
Good Fortune.

My research revealed that lucky people do not
achieve their dreams and ambitions purely by chance.
Nor does fate conspire to prevent unlucky people
from obtaining what they want. Instead, lucky and
unlucky people achieve, or fail to achieve, their
ambitions because in a fundamental difference in
how they think about both themselves and their lives.

The concept can be illustrated with a simple example. Earlier on in the book we met lucky competition winners Lynne, Joe and Wendy. All of them won a huge number of prizes, and all put much of their good luck down to the fact that they enter a large number of competitions. As Joe said, "You have to be in to win." Many of the unlucky people explained that they never entered competitions and lotteries because they were convinced that their bad luck would prevent them from winning. As Lucy, a 23-year-old unlucky student, told me:

I can remember, even when I was little, not entering things because I just never won anything. When I was seven, I was at primary school in an assembly and my parents were in the audience. My mum had entered a competition for me and they called out the winner and it was me. But I hadn't entered it, it was my mum. The way I see it, I hadn't won, she had.

Clearly, unlucky people's expectations about competitions are very likely to become self-fulfilling prophecies. By not entering competitions, they severely reduce their chances of winning, and exactly the same attitude affects many important areas of their life. The resulting lack of any attempt to change their lives can easily turn unlucky people's low expectations about the future into a miserable reality.

Extract from *THE LUCK FACTOR* by Richard Wiseman published by Century/Arrow. Used by permission of The Random House Group Limited.

*"**Definition of the Law of Attraction**: I attract to my life whatever I give my energy, focus, and attention to, whether wanted or unwanted."*
Michael Losier

The Law of Attraction

The law of attraction concept was introduced to me by a colleague. I found the idea a bit odd at first and the more I read, the more I liked the notion that I could be lucky and be a winner by feeling lucky and feeling like a winner. Try it and see what happens.

We create by feeling, not by thought!

That's right, we get what we get by the way we feel, not by trying to slug things into place or control our minds. Every car accident, job promotion, great or lousy lover, full or empty bank account comes to us by the most elemental law of physics: like attracts like. And since most of us haven't felt too hot about what we've had for most of our lives, we've become highly gifted masters at attracting an overabundance of circumstances we'd rather not have.

You want a new car? You got it! You want to work successfully for yourself? You got it! You want to close that deal? Make more money? Have a great relationship? Live without fear? Have a spiritually fulfilling life? Have superb health, freedom, independence? You got it, *if* you know how to f*eeee*l it into being.

The Law of Attraction—like attracts like—is absolute (and has nothing to do with personalities). No one lives beyond this law, for it is the law of the universe. It's just that we never realized until recently that the law applies to us too. This is the law behind success or failure. It's what causes fender-benders or fatalities. It is, to the point, what runs every waking moment of our lives.

So if we want to turn our lives around, or bring in greater abundance, or health, or safety, or happiness of any kind, we have only to learn the simple steps of

170

manipulating our "feelings," and a whole new world of plenty opens for the asking.

But the greatest obstacle to living our potential comes from toddler days when we were trained to look for what's wrong—with everything! With our jobs, our cars, our relationships, our clothes, our shapes, our health, our freeways, our planet, our faith, our entertainment, our children, our government, even our friends. Yet most of the world can't even agree about what right or wrong is, so we war, and strike, and demonstrate, and make laws, and go to psychiatrists.

"That's life," you say. "We have to take the good with the bad, the ups with the downs. We have to on guard, work hard, do things right, be watchful and hope for a break. Yes, that's the way life is."

No, no, and NO! That is simply not the way real Life is, and it's time we faced up to how we actually do create what we have in our world, our empty or full bank accounts, our grand or boring jobs, our good fortune or bad, and everything else in this arena we so nonchalantly call reality.

How do we do it? Don't laugh; it all comes from...*how we're vibrating!*

Everything in this world is made of energy: you, me, the rock, the table, the blades of grass. And since energy is actually vibration, that means that everything that exists vibrates. Everything! Including you and me.

Modern-day physicists have finally come to agree that energy and matter are one and the same, which brings us back to where we started: that everything vibrates, because everything—whether you can see it or not—is energy. Pure, pulsing, ever-flowing energy.

But even though there's only one energy, it vibrates differently. Just like the sound that pours out of a musical instrument, some energy vibrates fast (such as high notes) from high frequencies, and some vibrates slow (such as low notes) from low frequencies. Unlike the tones from a musical instrument, however, the energy that flows out from us comes from our highly charged emotions to create highly charged *electromagnetic* wave patterns of energy, making us powerful—but volatile—walking magnets.

That's nice, but who cares? Well, if you want to know why you've had to struggle so hard with your life, you do! If you want to know how to change your life to be exactly the way you want it to be, you had darn well better care, because the electromagnetic vibrations you send out every split second of every day are what have brought—and are continuing to bring—everything onto your life, big or small, good or bad. Everything! *No exceptions.*

Reprinted with the permission of Hampton Roads Publishing Company, Inc., 434-296-2772, www.hrpub.com, from *Excuse Me, Your Life is Waiting* by Lynn Grabhorn. Copyright © 2000 by Lynn Grabhorn

"The Law of Attraction does not respond to the words you use or the thoughts you think. It simply responds to how you feel about what you say and what you think."
Michael Losier

There are some actions you can take to begin vibrating to attract what you *do* want, as opposed to what you *don't* want.

SELF TALK
A Self Talk is an expression we use as a statement of truth. It can be positive or negative and it often made unconsciously. It can also be called your inner voice.

Negative Self Talk
- I'll have to work hard to make good money.
- I never win the lottery.
- I'll never lose the weight I want.
- Good women/men are hard to find.
- Money come in one hand and goes out the other.
- It's hard to get clients during the summer.
- I take one step forward and two steps back.
- My business slows down during the holidays.

Complaining and worrying are negative statements. Every time you complain about something, you're giving more attention to what you don't like. When you worry about the future, you're giving more attention to what you don't want.

Positive Self Talk
- I'm lucky, because I always find money.
- I always find work and clients easily.
- Everything I touch turns to gold.
- I make friends easily.
- Money comes to me at the right time.
- I always get a great parking spot.

At this point, you're probably asking yourself how you can stop your pattern of negative thinking. The answer comes in the act of rephrasing what you think and what you say.

HOW TO REPHRASE NEGATIVE SELF TALK
As you become more aware of your use of language and its importance in your vibration, you will begin to catch yourself whenever you make a negative statement. When you hear it, turn the negative into a positive by restating what you have just said. Preface your sentence with "in the past." For example, if you hear yourself say, "It's hard to find clients," rephrase it by saying, "In the past, it was hard to find clients."

Copyright ©2003 by Michael Losier. Used by permission. www.michaellosier.com or www.lawofattractionbook.com

TIP: Keep a memory box and/or a spreadsheet of all your wins. I have a memory box that I keep all the congratulatory letters, ticket stubs, pictures, etc. in. I also keep a spreadsheet tracking all of our wins. Whenever I feel we are having a "dry" spell, I pull out the box or look at the spreadsheet and I instantly feel happy and lucky.

"Be aware of wonder. Live a balanced life - learn some and think some and draw and paint and sing and dance and play and work every day some."
Robert Fulghum

Energy Balancing: Inside & Out

qi (chē)
n. the circulating life energy that in Chinese philosophy is thought to be inherent in all things; in traditional Chinese medicine the balance of negative and positive forms in the body is believed to be essential for good health

Qi in English is often spelled as **chi** or **ch'i**. The Japanese form is **ki**.

Chi is a fundamental concept of everyday Chinese culture, most often defined as "air" or "breath" (for example, the colloquial Mandarin Chinese term for "weather" is *tiān qi*, or the "breath of heaven") and, by extension, "life force" or "spiritual energy" that is part of everything that exists. References to *chi* or similar philosophical concepts as a type of metaphysical energy that sustains living beings are used in many belief systems, especially in Asia.

The c*hi* is what needs to be in perfect balance within and around us to not only attract winnings but to have a joyous and prosperous life. I feel this is what has helped me get to where I am today, not only with contesting, but in life.

There are many ways to balance our inner and outer lives; meditation, visualization, yoga, *tai chi*, acupuncture, massage, *reiki*, and *feng shui*. This is a very short list of the types of activities and practices you can participate in to balance your life, your body, your family, your home, **YOU**.

Most of these balancing activities and practices have been around, within different cultures, for thousands of years. Many are becoming "mainstream" as our modern culture begins to incorporate ancient customs into our daily lives.

There are hundreds of books and websites that discuss each of these activities, practices and more in great detail. I will give you a very brief overview on two topics: 1) *chakras*, for balancing the inside and 2) *feng shui*, for balancing the outside. There are further resources to be found at the end of this book, on my website, at your local bookstore and on the Internet.

Inside

What's a *Chakra*?
Chakra is a Sanskrit word meaning wheel, or vortex, and it refers to each of the seven energy centers of which our consciousness, our energy system, is composed.

These *chakras*, or energy centers, function as pumps or valves, regulating the flow of energy through our energy system. The functioning of the *chakras* reflects decisions we make concerning how we choose to respond to conditions in our life. We open and close these valves when we decide what to think, and what to feel, and through which perceptual filter we choose to experience the world around us.

The *chakras* are not physical. They are aspects of consciousness in the same way that the auras are aspects of consciousness. The *chakras* are more dense than the auras, but not as dense as the physical body. They interact with the physical body through two major vehicles, the endocrine system and the nervous system. Each of the seven *chakras* is associated with one of the seven endocrine glands, and also with a group of nerves called a plexus. Thus, each *chakra* can be associated with particular parts of the body and particular functions within the body controlled by that plexus or that endocrine gland associated with that *chakra*.

All of your senses, all of your perceptions, all of your possible states of awareness, everything it is possible for you to experience, can be divided into seven categories. Each category can be associated with a particular *chakra*. Thus, the *chakras* represent not only particular parts of your physical body, but also particular parts of your consciousness.

When you feel tension in your consciousness, you feel it in the *chakra* associated with that part of your consciousness experiencing the stress, and in the parts of the physical body associated with that *chakra*. Where you feel the stress depends upon why you feel the stress. The tension in the *chakra* is detected by the nerves of the plexus associated with that *chakra*, and transmitted to the parts of the body controlled by that plexus. When the tension continues over a period of time, or to a particular level of intensity, the person creates a symptom on the physical level.

The symptom speaks a language that reflects the idea that we each create our reality, and the metaphoric significance of the symptom becomes apparent when the symptom is described from that point of view. Thus, rather than saying, "I can't see," the person would describe it as keeping themselves from seeing something. "I can't walk," means the person has been keeping themselves from walking away from a situation in which they are unhappy. And so on.

The symptom served to communicate to the person through their body what they had been doing to themselves in their consciousness. When the person changes something about their way of being, getting the message communicated by the symptom, the symptom has no further reason for being, and it can be released, according to whatever the person allows themselves to believe is possible.

We believe everything is possible.

We believe that anything can be healed. It's just a question of how to do it. Understanding the *chakras* allows you to understand the relationship between your consciousness and your body, and to thus see your body as a map of your consciousness. It gives you a better understanding of yourself and those around you.

What else is there?

Reprinted with permission by The Brofman Foundation for the Advancement of Healing. www.healer.ch

Another good site to visit is Sacred Centers
http://sacredcenters.com/chakras.html. They also have good
descriptions of what each *chakra* is and what it relates to.

> *"What we call luck is the inner man externalized.*
> *We make things happen to us."*
> Robertson Davies

Outside

Feng Shui: The art of studying the environment and how energies
interact with a home or premise. *Feng Shui* can hasten fulfillment of a
good destiny and give a better quality to life.

Feng Shui.
The Design & Organization of Space to Support Success

For thousands of years wise men and women have
been designing and organizing space to create an
environment that will support them to succeed in all
their endeavors. This type of design appears in all
cultures if we look back in history far enough.
Although it has been lost to many in the modern
western culture of North America, where hard
scientific fact has replaced gut instinct, (that voice
deep inside us that tells us we are on the right track).
However, a renaissance is taking place in North
America and this type of "Earth Wisdom" is now
surfacing in all forms of design.

Wealth or abundance in life comes in many forms
and means something different to each individual.
One of the great mysteries in life is why some people
attract more luck or success than others. One of the
keys to the success of these individuals is they truly
believe they cannot fail. They attract successful
energy to themselves because failure is not a word in

their vocabulary, to use a very trite phrase *"when life hands them a lemon they make lemonade"*. This attitude is one of the first and most important ingredients in creating living and working space that actively encourages you to succeed as opposed to actively encouraging you to fail.

In the hundreds of *Feng Shui* consultations I have done and clients I have met, the ones that have had the most success in all aspects of their lives are the ones that have had *"faith"*. They truly believed in their own ability and the ability of their environment to actively support them in achieving their goals. We call this good or positive *Chi*.

People naturally gravitate towards an individual who makes them feel good and people who feel good about themselves want to make other people feel good, it's a natural instinct to want to share positive *Chi*. How do we become one of those people who exude this winning energy, this positive attitude that says *"I can't fail"*? An exercise I give to my clients to prepare themselves for this attitude change is, every morning when you wake up you look in the mirror and you repeat over to yourself, *"Damn I'm Good"* if you repeat this phrase often enough over a period of time you will come to believe it. This is not ego; it is an exercise that builds up positive *chi*, self confidence and a sense of self worth. This is the first step in creating bountiful *Chi* that will support you to succeed in your life. It will put you on the road to becoming a winner.

The second step to creating a bountiful life is to use the space you live and work in to support your new found belief in a winning attitude. The greatest gift we can give ourselves and it costs us nothing except our effort, is to create an environment in our home or work place that continually says to us *"I am a*

179

winner". How do we physically go about doing this?

First look around the space you occupy and make sure there is room for you to function in it. One of the scenarios I see the most frequently when I visit clients is that there is so much furniture and *"stuff"* surrounding them that there is literally no physical room for the client. Go through every cupboard, closet and shelf in your home and office and ask your self three questions about the "stuff" you find there. 1. Do I need it? 2. Do I love it? 3. Do I use it? If the answer to these questions is no then "loose it".

How many of us have clothes in our closet we are keeping because as soon as we shed those extra ten or twenty pounds, we will get back into them but for whatever reason the pounds seem to hang around in the same way the clothes do. Well get rid of the clothes, give them away and if you shed the pounds go out and buy yourself some new ones to celebrate your success.

Live with what you love. Don't hang on to anything furniture, jewelry, artwork, knick-knacks etc. that doesn't make you feel good about yourself, no matter who gave them to you. Every time you look at the article, it gives you a negative message. This is particularly true for past relationships. Don't keep the marital bed or dinning room table after a divorce; in fact don't keep anything from a failed relationship that will remind you of past mistakes or pain.

The third step to creating bountiful space that will support your success is to pay careful attention to where you enter and exit your home or office. The front door or main entry to any home or office is the one designated by the architect, no matter if you always use the mudroom or back door. The main entry should be used as frequently as possible and a clear people path from the road or driveway should lead to this door. This is the area of your home or office where all the beneficial Chi that enters your life will come through. Your entry is where you welcome your friends, family, but most importantly yourself to your home, it should bring a smile to your face every time you come through the door. This is where you would place your favorite piece of artwork, a beautiful vase or rug. You have one opportunity to make a first impression and this is where you place your best effort.

Many of us in North America enter and exit our homes through the garage or mudroom. If this is the case for you then you would also turn your attention to these areas of your home. This is not the place to pile up a mountain of dirty laundry, or the place where the first thing you see when you enter your home is the kitty litter box. Cat poop and dirty laundry are hardily inspiring things to view or to use to support a winning attitude, as you enter and exit your paradise. One idea for using this area to support your goals is to turn it into a rogue's gallery, hang pictures of family or friends on the walls or use them to showcase the artwork of your children or grandchildren.

I love to tell the story of the client who painted a spa on her garage wall, it was the last thing she saw before heading to work and the first she saw on returning home. She credited the positive energy she gained from this mural for increasing the bottom line of her company by twenty percent and her employees and clients reported it made a huge difference in a very positive way on how she handled her business dealings. This was a perfect example of using space to stimulate a winning attitude.

This gives us just a brief glimpse of how we can use

our space to support our success, we all have different strategies for creating a winning mind set and stimulating positive *Chi*, we can create a whole new view of ourselves and our lives.

Norah Higgerty is an International Feng Shui Consultant. Based in New Brunswick, she can be reached at higgerty@nb.sympatico.ca

"The universe operates through dynamic exchange... giving and receiving are different aspects of the flow of energy in the universe. And in our willingness to give that which we seek, we keep the abundance of the universe circulating in our lives."
Deepak Chopra

You Get What You Give

It is my personal observation that the people that post the most contests, help others with answers and in general, share, seem to post the most wins. This principle goes back thousands of years. (see *Join an Online Community*.)

Deepak Chopra wrote a book, *The Seven Spiritual Laws of Success*. I feel that law number two, The Law of Giving, helps describe my theory; *the more I share, the more I win*. Statistically, the opposite should be true. The more people that enter a contest should decrease my odds of winning. However, I believe the opposite to be true, "I can't lose helping others win".

I share/post as many contests, answers, and help as often as I can to as many groups as I can. I know there are people within those groups entering many more contests than I do. Yet, in 2004 *and* 2005 I won 100+ contests. Why do I win 5, 10, 15+ contests every month (month after month)? Why have I not paid for a trip in four years? I believe it directly ties into The Law of Giving.

That is why you must give and receive in order to keep wealth and affluence—or anything you want in life—circulating in your life.

The word affluence comes from the root word "*affluere*," which means "to flow to." The word affluence means "to flow in abundance." Money is really a symbol of the life energy we exchange and the life energy we use as a result of the service we provide to the universe. Another word for money is "currency," which also reflects the flowing nature of energy. The word currency comes from the Latin word "*currere*" which means "to run" or to flow.

Therefore, if we stop the circulation of money—if our only intention is to hold on to our money and hoard it—since it is life energy, we will stop its circulation back into our lives as well. In order to keep that energy coming to us, we have to keep the energy circulating. Like a river, money must keep flowing, otherwise it begins to stagnate, to clog, to suffocate and strangle its very own life force. Circulation keeps it alive and vital.

Every relationship is one of give and take. Giving engenders receiving, and receiving engenders giving. What goes up must come down; what goes out must come back. In reality, receiving is the same thing as giving, because giving and receiving are different aspects of the flow of energy in the universe. And if you stop the flow of either, you interfere with nature's intelligence.

The more you give, the more you will receive, because you will keep the abundance of the universe circulating in your life. In fact, anything that is of value in life only multiplies when it is given. That which doesn't multiply through giving is neither worth giving nor worth receiving. If, through the act of giving, you feel you have lost something, then the gift is not truly given and will not cause increase. If you give grudgingly, there is no energy behind that giving.

It is the intention behind your giving and receiving that is the most important thing. The intention should always be to create happiness for the giver and receiver, because happiness is life-supporting and life-sustaining and therefore generates increase. The return is directly proportional to the giving when it is unconditional and from the heart. That is why the act of giving has to be joyful—the frame of mind has to be one in which you feel joy in the very act of giving. Then the energy behind the giving increases many times over.

Practicing the *Law of Giving* is actually very simple: if you want joy, give joy to others; if you want love, learn to give love; if you want attention and appreciation, learn to give attention and appreciation; if you want material affluence, help others to become materially affluent. In fact, the easiest way to get what you want is to help others get what they want. This principle works equally well for individuals, corporations, societies, and nations. If you want to be blessed with all the good things in life learn to silently bless everyone with all the good things in life.

From the book *The Seven Spiritual Laws of Success* © 1994, Deepak Chopra. Reprinted by permission of Amber-Allen Publishing, Inc. P.O. Box 6657, San Rafael, CA 94903. All rights reserved.

"Every action generates a force of energy that returns to us in like kind...what we sow is what we reap. And when we choose actions that bring happiness and success to others, the fruit of our karma is happiness and success."
Deepak Chopra

Good Karma

Galatians 6:7 Do not be deceived. God will not be made a fool. **For a person will reap what he sows,** 6:8 because the person who sows to his own flesh will reap corruption from the flesh, but the one who sows to the Spirit will reap eternal life from the Spirit.

The bible states you reap what you sow. You sow good fortune for others; you reap good fortune for yourself. This also ties back into the Law of Attraction—like attracting like.

I believe the expression *"cheaters never win."* You may cheat, and you may win that particular contest, but you will lose somewhere else in your life. It is not worth cheating.

Gary Zukav spoke eloquently in his book Soul Stories about how the cycle of getting what you give ties us with the Universe.

Another gift that you get from the Universe is an experience that is perfect for you. This gift comes each moment from the time you were born until you die.

You and the Universe create this gift together. You decide what it will be, and the Universe gives it to you. That is the Golden Rule—what you do to people, people do to you. It is also called karma. If you don't like what people do to you, you can change that by doing things different to them. That is how you and the Universe work together. Each moment you choose a new gift, and, when the time is right, the Universe gives it to you.

Each day brings gifts that you have ordered, and each day you place more orders. You do this by setting you intentions, and then acting on them. The Universe takes your orders, and delivers them. Everyone gets what she or he ordered. If you order fear, you get it. If you order love, you get it.

When you order, you share with the Universe. When your order is filled, the Universe shares with you. Complaining about your gifts is walking in the fog. Recognizing your gifts—and who ordered them—is walking in the sunshine.

Walking in the sunshine is clarity.

Reprinted with the permission of Simon & Schuster Adult Publishing Group from *SOUL STORIES* by Gary Zukav. Copyright © 2000 by Gary Zukav

"The Universe rewards action."
Jack Canfield

Just do it!

I enter almost every contest I come across. (I would enter more except I do not have the time.) In sales it is called a numbers game. The more prospects you call on, the more sales you are going to make. Similarly, I believe the more contests I enter, the more contests I am going to win.

Making Your Own Luck

Lynne's luck started when she happened to come across a newspaper article describing how a woman had won several impressive competition prizes. Lynne therefore decided to enter a crossword competition and won £10. A few weeks later she entered another competition and won three sports bikes. Shortly afterwards, she went to an interview for a position teaching an evening class in fashion design. There was a coffee jar on the interviewer's desk and it had a competition entry form on it. Lynne was drawn to this and asked if she could have the label. The interviewer asked why she wanted it and Lynne told her about how she had won some competitions. The interviewer asked her to come teach two evening classes—one on fashion design and one on how to win competitions. Lynne accepted the offer and also started to enter lots more competitions. Her winning streak continued and she won lots more prizes, including two cars and several holidays abroad.

Interestingly, these competition wins allowed Lynne to achieve her lifelong ambition of becoming a freelance writer. In 1992 she wrote a book on winning competitions. To publicise the book, a press release was sent to her local paper and they published an article about her work. The next day, the story was picked up by the national newspapers and she was invited to appear on several television shows. As a result, Lynne was invited to write newspaper articles on winning competitions. In 1996 she received a phone call from a major daily newspaper. They had seen her work and asked her to write a daily competition column for them. Her column, "Win with Lynne", was highly successful and ran for many years.

Lynne has fulfilled many of her lifelong ambitions, been happily married for over forty years and has a wonderful family life. Like many people involved in my research, Lynne attributes much of her success to good fortune.

Wendy is a 40-year-old housewife. She considers herself lucky in many aspects of her life, but is especially fortunate when it comes to winning competitions. On average, she wins about three prizes a week. Some of these prizes are quite small, but many have been substantial. In the last five years she has won large cash prizes and several major holidays abroad. Wendy certainly seems to have a magical ability to win competitions - and she is not the only one. In the previous chapter I described how Lynne has won several large prizes in competitions, including several cars and holidays.

The same is also true of Joe. Like both Wendy and Lynne, Joe considers himself to be very lucky in many areas of his life. He has been happily married for forty years and has a loving family. However, Joe is especially lucky in competitions, and his recent successes include winning televisions, a day spent on the set of a well-known television soap opera, and several holidays.

What is behind Lynne, Wendy and Joe's winning ways? Their secret is surprisingly simple. They all enter a very large number of competitions.

Each week, Wendy enters about sixty postal competitions, and about seventy Internet-based competitions. Likewise, both Lynne and Joe enter about fifty competitions a week, and their chances of winning are increased with each and every entry. All three of them were well aware that their lucky winning ways are, in reality, due to the large number of competitions they enter. As Wendy explained, "I am a lucky person, but luck is what you make it. I win a lot of competitions and prizes, but I do put a huge amount of effort into it." Joe commented:

People always said to me they think I'm very lucky because of the amount of competitions that I win. But then they tell me that they don't enter many themselves, and I think, "Well, if you don't enter, you have no chance of winning." They look at me as being very lucky, but I think you make your own luck ... as I say to them "You've got to be in to win."

Extract from *THE LUCK FACTOR* by Richard Wiseman published by Century/Arrow. Used by permission of The Random House Group Limited.

"Winning is important to me, but what brings me real joy is the experience of being fully engaged in whatever I'm doing."
Phil Jackson

CONCLUSION

STORY: Lynn was a very special woman who was as passionate about contesting as I am. Sadly Lynn passed away in 2005 and I feel she has handed down her crown and title of "Contest Queen" to me. I wanted to share with you Lynn's luckiest day.

80CR

One of the most exciting days of my life was the day I started getting dressed to go and pick-up the car I had won. My husband called and while we were talking the "call waiting beep" warned me another call was on the line. It was a judging agency asking me to answer a skill testing question. I answered correctly so they informed me I won a trip to Greece. Ken was still on hold so I excitedly told him about my latest win. As we were talking the mail man arrived with a registered letter informing me I had won a trip to Mexico! You can imagine Ken's surprise when I told him I just won a second trip to Mexico. A car and two trips all in one day! I'm still working on topping that one.

Extract from *WINNING WAYS* by Lynn Banks Goutbeck and Melanie Rockett. Used by permission of Proof Positive Productions Ltd. www.proofpositive.com

80CR

If you were new to contesting when you began reading this book I hope I have turned you into a savvy contestor. If you were a seasoned contestor, I hope I have helped you learn a few tips, tricks and about the new technologies. My goal when I began writing this book was to teach people about the hobby of contesting and hopefully, have as much fun as I do dreaming, entering and winning.

And remember, *you can't win if you don't enter*.
GOOD LUCK & HAVE FUN!!

RECOMMENDED READING

Advertising and Marketing Law in Canada
by Brenda Pritchard and Susan Vogt

Canada boasts one of the most highly regulated advertising environments in the world, with specific federal and provincial legislation as well as scores of self-regulatory codes, policies and bodies. Without a solid understanding of the legal constraints, even the cleverest advertising or marketing campaign can run aground on legal technicalities.

Written by two of Canada's leading advertising and marketing lawyers, *Advertising and Marketing Law in Canada* is a powerful resource which lays out the legal issues in a clear and accessible way, identifies pitfalls and potential problem areas in marketing and advertising programs, provides a wide variety of real world examples to illustrate practical points, delivers straightforward analysis of the regulatory regime, highlights best practices, and underlines important "do's and don'ts".

Topics covered include: drawing the line on false representations and misleading advertising, pricing issues, protecting intellectual property, using different marketing channels, dealing with talent and negotiating effective contracts, packaging and labelling restrictions, marketing to children, running contests and promotions, and the sale of natural health products.

Contest Guru's Guide to Winning Sweepstakes
by Melanie Rockett*

Your guide to an exciting and lucrative hobby.
Find out:
- What makes sweepstakes different from a raffle, from a lottery.
- Where to find sweepstakes.

- Links to the best offline and online newsletters.
- What laws govern contests, sweeps, etc. (the US & Canada).
- What an HDF is and how to create one.
- How to draw UPC codes.
- How to get organized for off line contesting.
- Tools for online contesting.
- Links to the best sweeps sites.
- Where to find contests.
- The FOUR winning ways Secrets.
- Meet some BIG winners.
- Do contest winners pay taxes?
- Contesting tools and resources.
- How the principles of attraction can help you create LUCK.
  ...and more!

Download your FREE COPY of Contest Guru while it is still free. Visit www.contestguru.com, sign up for the newsletter and the book is yours!

* NOTE: Melanie co-wrote Winning Ways with Lynn Goutbeck.

Excuse Me, Your *Life* is Waiting
by Lynn Grabhorn

*never before told, because it
was never before known*

In an upbeat, humorous, and somewhat irreverent style, Lynn Grabhorn introduces us to the amazing Law of Attraction, a new and rapidly unfolding realm of feelings that physicians, scientists, physicists, and theologians are coming to believe is very, very real.

Excuse Me, Your LIFE Is Waiting clarifies why most of our dreams have never materialized, why the majority of us have lived with all-too-empty bank accounts, tough relationships, failing health, and often spiritually unfulfilling lives. Most importantly, in an easy-to-read style peppered with logical explanations, simple steps, and true-life

194

examples, Lynn Grabhorn shows us how to turn it all around—right now.

The most unconscious thing we do all day long is what actually creates and molds every moment of every day of our lives. And what is this "thing" that governs us so forcefully? Feelings! Grabhorn reveals how our feelings make our lives what they are—not positive thinking, or sweat and strain, or good or bad luck, or even smarts, but feelings: good ones, bad ones, up ones, down ones, and all the ones in between.

Until now, we have run our lives on a default setting, manifesting experiences by happenstance rather than intent. Now, with no effort other than paying attention to how we're feeling, the play becomes our deliberate creation, and the world becomes our oyster.

How to Win Lotteries Sweepstakes and Contests in the 21st Century (2nd Edition)
by Steve Ledoux

Learn the Winning Secrets of America's Sweepstakes King!
In this completely revised and updated second edition of his best-selling book (over 75,000 copies sold!), Steve Ledoux reveals the secrets that have enabled him to win thousands and thousands of dollars in cash and prizes. He also shares his skills in choosing lottery numbers, entering and winning sweepstakes and contests, and spotting illegal scams in this savvy collection of prize-winning strategies.

Lottery and sweepstakes hopefuls learn how to find the right contests to enter, how to protect themselves from cheaters, and what to expect after winning, including how to deal with the IRS and give interviews to the media. Internet sweepstakes, contests, game shows, and resources complete this guide to winning the jackpot!

Steve Ledoux has won more then 500 sweepstakes and contests and has collected thousands and thousands of dollars in winnings. He has been a winning contestant on Wheel of Fortune, has won all-expenses-paid trips for two to the Caribbean, Hawaii, Jamaica, and Las Vegas, and has won a year's supply of Ben & Jerry's ice cream.

Law of Attraction
by Michael Losier

You're Already Experiencing the Law of Attraction

You may not be aware of it, but a very powerful force is at work in your life. It's called the Law of Attraction and right now it's attracting people, jobs, situations, and relationships to your life—not all of them good! If your life feels as if it's turned south and taken on the characteristics of a bad soap opera, it's time to pick up this book.

This complete how-to reference will teach you how to make the Law of Attraction work for you by helping you eliminate the unwanted from your life and filling it up with the things that give you energy, prosperity, and joy.

You can use the Law of Attraction to make a few changes in your life or do a complete overhaul. You'll find all the directions right here. Discover how easy it is to use the Law of Attraction to:
- Stop attracting things you don't want.
- Increase wealth.
- Find your perfect mate.
- Increase your customer base.
- Clarify your goals and strategies.
- Locate your ideal job.

The Luck Factor
by Richard Wiseman

The revolutionary book that reveals the four scientific principles of luck - and how you can use them to change your life

For over ten years, psychologist Professor Richard Wiseman has been conducting a unique research project, examining the behaviour of over a thousand volunteers who considered themselves `lucky' or `unlucky'. The results reveal a radical new way of looking at luck:
- You hold the key to creating your luck.

- There are four simple behavioural techniques that are scientifically proven to help you attract good fortune.
- You can use these principles to revolutionize every area of your life - including your relationships, personal finances and career.

For the first time, the elusive luck factor has been identified. Using the simple techniques described in this book, you can learn how to increase your levels of luck, confidence and success.

The Power of Positive Thinking
by Norman Vincent Peale

> *"This book is written with the sole objective of helping the reader achieve a happy, satisfying, and worthwhile life."*
> *Dr. Norman Vincent Peale*

This classic book will help you to learn how to:
- Break the worry habit.
- Get other people to like you.
- "Energize your life"—to give yourself the vitality and initiative needed to carry out your ambitions and hopes.
- Avoid "the jitters" in your daily work.
- Believe in yourself and in everything you do.
- Live a controlled, relaxed life no matter how fast the pace may be.
- Build a new power and determination through a simple formula that really works.
- Develop the power to reach your goals.
- Think the kind of thoughts that lead you to a fuller life and satisfying success.

Faith in Yourself Makes Good Things Happen to You

197

The Prize Winner of Defiance, Ohio
by Terry Ryan

The Prize Winner of Defiance, Ohio introduces Evelyn Ryan, an enterprising woman who kept poverty at bay with wit, poetry and perfect prose during the "contest era" of the 1950s and 1960s. Evelyn's winning ways defied the church, her alcoholic husband, and antiquated views of housewives. To her, flouting convention was a small price to pay when it came to raising her six sons and four daughters.

Graced with a rare appreciation for life's inherent hilarity, Evelyn turned every financial challenge into an opportunity for fun and profit. The story of the irrepressible woman, whose clever entries are worthy of Erma Bombeck, Dorothy Parker, and Ogden Nash, is told by her daughter terry with an infectious joy that shows how a winning spirit will always triumph over poverty.

Soul Stories
by Gary Zukav

Writing with profound psychological and spiritual insight, prizewinning author Gary Zukav has had a major impact on the consciousness of millions. In his *New York Times* number-one best seller, *The Seat of the Soul*, he explained how the expansion of human perception beyond the five senses leads to a new understanding of power—the alignment of the personality with the soul—which in turn leads to an awareness of our extraordinary creative abilities. Now, in one of the most important and useful books you will ever read, Soul Stories, Zukav shows how this new understanding of power—authentic power—transforms lives in countless ways.

Soul Stories is filled with marvelous stories that show how concepts such as intuition, harmony, cooperation, sharing, and reverence for life actually express themselves in people's lives. Best of all, the stories lead to practical advice on how you can discover your own Soul Stories and the truths they reveal about the deepest sources of your being. Wonderfully readable, *Soul Stories* is a wise and inspirational book.

The Seven Spiritual Laws of Success
by Deepak Chopra

This is a book you will cherish for a lifetime, for within its pages are the secrets to making all your dreams come true. In *The Seven Spiritual Laws of Success*, Deepak Chopra distills the essence of his teachings into seven simple, yet powerful principles that can easily be applied to create success in all areas of your life.

Based on natural laws which govern all of creation, this book shatters the myth that success is the result of hard work, exacting plans, or driving ambition.

In *The Seven Spiritual Laws of Success,* Deepak Chopra offers a life-altering perspective on the attainment of success: Once we understand our true nature and learn to live in harmony with natural law, a sense of well-being, good health, fulfilling relationships, energy and enthusiasm for life, and material abundance will spring forth easily and effortlessly.

Filled with timeless wisdom and practical steps you can apply right away, this is a book you will want to read and refer to again and again.

Surreal Gourmet Bites: show-stoppers and conversation starters
by Bob Blumer

With Surreal Gourmet Bites, Bob Blumer elevates party food into wow-inspiring, how-did-you-think-of-that creations.

It's no wonder Bob's called The Surreal Gourmet. He's an artist when it comes to food. And these little masterpieces are as lighthearted as the party itself: Chinese Snow Cones (chicken salad with ginger vinaigrette in baked wonton cones); Coconut Shrimp Lollypops (coconut-crusted shrimp with an apricot-ginger dipping sauce); S'mores Shooters (amaretto hot chocolate with roasted marshmallows). Each recipe comes complete with ways to simplify the dish, level of skill needed, prep times, and even suggestions for music to cook by and beverage pairings. Pick one or two to set the stage for an impressive dinner or several for a fabulous cocktail party that will keep your guests talking about the food all the way home.

The beauty of Blumer's recipes is that they are foolproof—even for most culinary challenged cooks. They rely on ingredients found at the local grocery store that are brought to life with heavy-handed infusion of fresh herbs and spices. These whimsically presented bites are simple enough for impromptu gatherings, yet memorable enough to become addictive. With Surreal Gourmet Bites, the food will be the life of the party.

Bob Blumer is the creator and host of the Food Network Canada show The Surreal Gourmet. He lives in the Hollywood Hills where his other car is a Toastermobile. This is his fourth book.

Winning Sweepstakes: The Proven Strategy
by Jeffrey & Robin Sklar

Not all sweepstakes are created equal…Some are much easier to win than others. Learn how to recognize and win the best, most "winnable" ones!

Jeffrey and Robin Sklar, publishers of Winning Sweepstakes Newsletter, are nationally recognized authorities at winning sweepstakes. They wrote Winning Sweepstakes: The Proven Strategy to share the proven winning strategies they have developed since winning the first sweepstake they entered in 1981. Since then, the couple has won tens of thousands of dollars in sweepstakes prizes…not by sheer luck but rather by devoting their entries to the best sweepstakes with the best prizes and best odds of winning.

They are acknowledged as the first players to apply computing science to sweepstake playing and are sometimes referred to as "Mr. And Mrs. Sweepstakes" and the "Odds Couple". The Sklars and their sweepstakes successes have been featured on the Today Show, Nightline, the Wall Street Journal Report and in Money Magazine.

This book stands alone as the only comprehensive authoritative "how-to" source of information evaluating, entering and winning sweepstakes. Here are just a few of the hundreds of tips you'll learn:

- 13 ways to spot the easiest-to-win sweepstakes
- Which sweepstakes have terrible odds and are a waste of your time
- How to win unclaimed prizes in second chance sweepstakes
- Which industries consistently sponsor the best sweepstakes
- Exactly how many entries you need to win game sweepstakes
- How NOT to be among the up to 40% disqualified entries
- How to interpret the official rules
- 8 ways to make your contest entries more original
- How to maximize the edge against you in state lotteries
- Plus much, much more!

REMEMBER! To win regularly, it is not enough to enter often, you must ENTER SMART! Winning Sweepstakes: The Proven Strategy reveals how sweepstakes and contests work, and how to make the odds win for you!